THE CENTURY PSYCHOLOGY SERIES

Richard M. Elliott, Gardner Lindzey & Kenneth MacCorquodale
Editors

THE CHALLENGE OF
RESPONSE SETS

THE CENTURY PSYCHOLOGY SERIES AWARD
For 1964

Each year Appleton-Century-Crofts gives an award
for a distinguished manuscript in psychology selected by the Editors of the Century Psychology
Series. Considered will be works of two hundred
typed pages or longer, which provide a significant
contribution to the field of psychology.

EDITORS:

Richard M. Elliott
Gardner Lindzey
Kenneth MacCorquodale

1962 BERNARD RIMLAND
*Infantile Autism: The Syndrome and its Implications
for a Neural Theory of Behavior*
1963 EDWARD E. JONES
Ingratiation: A Social Psychological Analysis

The Challenge of
Response Sets

Unconfounding Meaning, Acquiescence,
and Social Desirability in the MMPI

JACK BLOCK
University of California, Berkeley

New York

APPLETON-CENTURY-CROFTS
DIVISION OF MEREDITH PUBLISHING COMPANY

PREFACE

This inquiry began almost casually. Whereupon the good fortune of abundant data and wondrous analytical possibilities lured me more and more deeply into an examination of certain questions about the structure and significance of personality inventories. In so doing, some results developed that place me squarely, and with little compromise against the interpretation of the MMPI in terms of distorting and psychologically uninteresting response sets. While I of course hope that my analyses and conclusions are compelling, I am also hopeful that the readers of this effort will respond to the spirit of analytical uncovering in which it was conceived.

I have incurred many debts along the way to the completion of this work. My primary obligation is to Eleanor Krasnow who developed the computer programs on which my analyses have depended. Besides constructing programs both versatile and simple to invoke, she responded most generously with her time and knowledge to the various special analytical requirements cropping up—usually on an emergency basis—as the goal of unconfounding was pursued. The computer time needed by this unfunded project was graciously made available by the Computer Center of the University of California.

Where the 704 and the 7090 proved intractable or inconvenient, the aid of two other digital computers was sought and must be duly acknowledged here. For their help in many of the tiresome clerical tasks required for the preparation of this monograph, I am grateful to Susan D. Block and Judith L. Block.

The courtesy of Jeanne Block, Curt Hardyck, and Gale Bach in providing some of the data samples studied in these analyses also earns my thanks.

My knowledge and sophistication with respect to the MMPI

improved greatly from talking with Robert E. Harris and from some conceptual arguments he advanced in criticism of an early version of this manuscript. I am most grateful to him. Leonard Rorer and Lewis Goldberg were a resource ready on short notice and from a long distance to provide an esoteric datum or note my errors. My wife Jeanne, besides providing her usual and necessary encouragements, has made many helpful suggestions directed toward clarifying the involved argument and shaping its style of presentation. Knowing full well the enormous number of calculations that have been executed for this enterprise, it is with some trepidation that I accept the full and final responsibility for the conclusions advanced here. Many have helped but the errors are mine.

A first version of this manuscript, containing the essential analyses, was completed in May, 1962 at the Institute of Human Development, University of California in Berkeley. This research was a by-product of support received from the National Institute of Mental Health at that time. The elaboration and final revision of the monograph occupied much of my year, 1963–1964, at the Institute of Social Research in Oslo, Norway where I held a United States Public Health Service Special Research Fellowship. I wish to record here my thanks to Erik Rinde, Director, and Dagfinn Ås, Associate Director, for making me feel at home during my foreign stay.

J. B.

Oslo, February, 1964

CONTENTS

THE CHALLENGE OF
RESPONSE SETS

1

INTRODUCTION AND SUMMARY

A number of recent articles have conjectured and finally concluded that the widely used Minnesota Multiphasic Personality
Inventory (MMPI) is most profitably to be interpreted in terms of
response sets rather than in terms of content. Two response
"styles," acquiescence [1] and desirability,[2] are championed as
necessary and perhaps sufficient dimensions for understanding
the MMPI. Demonstrations in support of these reinterpretations
have appeared frequently and have not, in the main, been coun-
tered. If only because of reiteration, there seems to be a growing
consensus in the literature that the more recent viewpoints represent an advance in understanding of what is being measured by
personality inventories. Because inventories have been, are, and
may be expected to be employed as fundamental measurement
tools in the realm of personality psychology, the radical revalua-
tion of such devices as the MMPI is a highly significant development warranting, in its turn, most careful examination.

The advent of these newer interpretations, however, has not
brought comfortable clarity and insight to the MMPI. Rather,
controversy has shifted its locus with arguments now about the
comparative primacy of these two response sets and the ability of

---

[1] The response "style" of acquiescence, as defined elsewhere (cf., Couch
& Keniston, 1960, p. 152) and as employed here and conventionally, refers
to the tendency of an individual to agree or say "yes" to personality inventory statements, regardless of the content of the items.

[2] The response set of social desirability is to be understood as the tendency
of an individual "to give socially desirable responses to items in personality
inventories, regardless of whether the socially desirable response is True or
False" (Edwards, 1959, p. 108).

the one response style to encompass the relationships claimed for the other. Thus, in commenting on the content-interpreted factor analysis reported by Kassebaum, Couch, and Slater (1959), Edwards and Heathers (1962) reinterpret the first MMPI factor as reflecting social desirability while Messick and Jackson (1961a) view the identical factor as signifying acquiescence. A measure Couch and Keniston (1960) put forward as an index of agreement-response set can be construed with equal plausibility as a measure of social undesirability, suggest Edwards and Walker (1961a). Whereupon Couch and Keniston (1961) call attention to the possible presence within Edwards' Social Desirability (*SD*) scale of a strong acquiescence component.

These notes of discord have not caused any retreat from the essential response-set position that the MMPI is best conceived in these newer terms. Although there continues to be disagreement about the relative importance and priority of social desirability and acquiescence, there is unanimity among the primary protagonists of these response sets that both emerge as significant factors within the MMPI (Edwards, Diers, & Walker, 1962; Couch & Keniston, 1961; Messick & Jackson, 1961a). For Edwards, the few relationships within the MMPI that are not due to the operation of the social desirability variable arise because items with neutral social desirability values are involved. With such items, he suggests that acquiescent tendencies may be operating (Edwards, 1961). For Messick and Jackson (1961a), the instance where an acquiescence interpretation encounters anomalous findings can be understood readily by invoking the additional response style of social desirability.

It is the purpose of the present monograph to contest the interpretation that "acquiescence, as moderated by social desirability, plays a dominant role in personality inventories like the MMPI" (Messick & Jackson, 1961a, p. 303). It will be argued that the beleaguered MMPI, though by modern standards a less than optimal personality inventory, is by no means as innocent of psychological meaning as response-set adherents have suggested. As corollaries of this assertion, which it is believed follows from the several analyses to be reported, it will be further contended that (1) acquiescent-response set is *not* a significant component underlying the MMPI and (2) the social desirability interpretation, although seemingly applicable in many MMPI contexts, has achieved its support for fortuitous and epiphenomenal reasons.

Our argument is involved and prolonged and it has seemed best to adopt the dialectical strategy of focusing in detail upon acquiescence before considering social desirability. The sequence of development is as follows:

First, the "clear evidence" for the acquiescence view is reviewed. The difficulties of establishing "pure" or content-free measures of acquiescence within the inventory domain are discussed and exemplified, with particular attention devoted to recent, hitherto unevaluated demonstrations of the acquiescence effect. The inescapable constraint on the evidential value of acquiescence demonstrations within the MMPI—namely, the admissibility of a content-basis for the results obtained—is shown to apply to studies previously thought to speak clearly for the acquiescence interpretation.

Second, it is observed that although acquiescence measures seem always to be vulnerable to an alternative interpretation in terms of content-dimensions, the converse of this situation does not apply. Content-relevant measures *can* be constructed which, beyond reasonable dispute, eliminate the possibility of an interpretation in terms of acquiescence. A simple way of revising *current* MMPI scales so that acquiescence-response style is fairly and completely prevented from intruding is described. Some empirical relationships in support of this approach to eliminate acquiescence within the MMPI are brought forward.

Third, it is shown, via factor analyses of five separate and different samples, that the first two factors of the MMPI—the factors held to be due to response sets—continue to exist and *in identical form* when the acquiescence component is completely removed from MMPI scales. This finding eliminates acquiescence from consideration as an important determinant of the respondent's behavior when confronted with the MMPI.

Fourth, with the acquiescence interpretation no longer viable as an interpretation of either of the first two MMPI factors, it is shown how certain intrinsic and in part accidental characteristics of the MMPI-item pool have permitted the possibility of an acquiescence interpretation to develop. The apparently multi-pronged empirical support of the acquiescence interpretation provided by different kinds of analyses can be seen to stem from these retrospectively regrettable but by no means vitiating properties of the MMPI pool of items.

Fifth, we shift to evaluate the social desirability interpretation of the MMPI. The concept, its operational specification, and the empirical findings organized by it are evaluated critically and found to be of ambiguous import because of a confounding of social desirability with equally tenable, characterological dimensions of explanation. Nevertheless, the collinearity of social desirability with the first and pervasively important Alpha factor of the MMPI remains unquestionable. Strictly speaking, the tenability and convenience of an interpretation of the MMPI under the social desirability rubric may be continued so long as this confounding exists, despite the heuristic failure of the SD hypothesis in other behavioral domains and despite the nature of the external correlates of the disputed dimension.

Sixth, an asymmetry in the possibilities of unconfounding is again noted. Although the social desirability interpretation of the first MMPI factor is afflicted by the concomitant presence of alternatives of a more psychodynamic nature, measurement of this factor can be achieved eliminating the influence of a social-desirability effect. An MMPI scale measuring the factor dimension collinear with the *SD* scale is constructed which is reliable, fully valid, but *desirability-free*. The feasibility of developing a desirability-free measure of "social desirability," by unconfounding the previously linked interpretations, demonstrates that the notion of social desirability is related only adventitiously to a personality dimension of fundamental behavioral significance.

Seventh, the personological significance of the first two, and basic, factors (now no longer permissibly construed as acquiescence or social desirability) is explored in five samples by resort to independently formulated assessments by judges of high and low scorers on these factor dimensions. The behavioral correlates of these MMPI dimensions are found to be numerous, of import, and to constellate in accord with previous content-based interpretations of these factors. An effort is made to identify these two factors in theoretical terms that envelop the specific empirical relationships while yet maintaining a larger conceptual fruitfulness. The problem of measuring these factor dimensions by currently available and by some newly developed scales is also briefly discussed.

Finally, some more general implications of these analyses and findings for personality assessment by structured inventories are drawn. The value of the MMPI and yet the present necessity to go beyond it is emphasized together with the suggestion that research on inventories become again referent to independent behaviors and outcomes. Internal analyses are useful, often required, and certainly seductive now that computers are widely available. But the world beyond inventories is the ultimate one and must be consulted for reassurance or chastening.

2

A NEGATIVE VIEW OF
ACQUIESCENCE RESEARCH

The history of concern with the acquiescence problem goes back
at least to Cady (1923), who attempted to reverse a number of
the questions in Woodworth's Personal Data Sheet (1918). In
1937, Lorge reported positive correlations between the number of
affirmative responses made by subjects on each of a variety of
temperament, attitude, and interest inventories. Lorge concluded
that "the tendency to respond by *Yes's, No's,* and *?'s* . . . may be
symptomatic of a special aspect of personality" (Lorge, 1937, p.
546), but his highest correlation, according to Cronbach (1950),
was .24.

Lentz (1938) introduced the term, "acquiescence," to identify
"the tendency to agree rather than disagree to . . . propositions
in general" (Lentz, 1938, p. 659). According to Lentz, "acquiescence may be a very distorting factor in the measurement of various other continui which call for positive and negative reactions
to propositions . . ." Only an abstract of this work, containing
neither details of method nor correlations found, has been published.

It was Cronbach's series of papers (1941; 1942; 1946; 1950)
which articulated the problem of acquiescent-response bias and
sensitized psychologists to the effects, both actual and potential,
of this source of response variance. Cronbach was concerned
largely with the effects of guessing or yes-no choice tendencies on
objective or achievement tests, where there is an objectively correct answer. He also developed the consequences of uncritical ac-

ceptance of item content within personality, attitude, or interest inventories, where the questions or items do not have a single correct answer. Rorer (1963) has aptly noted the distinction and, indeed, the logical independence of these two conceptions of acquiescence. It is the latter notion, of unthinking, content-inconsistent response to nonobjective items which has commanded the attention of most research since Cronbach's activation of interest in these problems.

The theme of acquiescence as a central (although still largely unanalyzed) determinant of inventory response has been applied persistently in the last ten years or so. Two sustained efforts stand out. These are:

1. The attempt to revalue the significance of the California F Scale designed to reflect authoritarianism (Adorno, Frenkel-Brunswik, Levison, & Sanford, 1950), conceiving of it primarily as an indicant of acquiescence;

2. The vigorously advanced reinterpretation of personality inventories, primarily the MMPI, as massive measures of acquiescent tendencies and other response biases instead of content-related psychological dimensions.

Our focus here must be upon the research and logical basis for this revisionism as it applies to the MMPI. However, it is instructive to detour briefly to consider the current status of the California F Scale after ten years of attempted assimilation by the acquiescence viewpoint.

Acquiescence and Authoritarianism After Ten Years

It is not well known that an imbalance of item phrasing in their scales was acknowledged by the authoritarianism researchers (Adorno *et al.*, 1950, p. 59). The scales were developed, not inadvertently, so that responses considered to be authoritarian required affirmative answers. Although recognized at the time as methodologically undesirable, this characteristic of the *F* and other authoritarianism-related scales was maintained since some efforts to design discriminating reversed items had proven unsuccessful. In abandoning the formal desideratum of response balance, it was presumed that the content of the *F* Scale items rather than the operant characteristics of the subject determined the scores he earned. By various inquiries into the characteristics of high and low scorers on their scales, the authoritarianism researchers built-up their case for the content-based validity of their scales as opposed to an interpretation in terms of response set.

The significance of this phrasing imbalance was then taken up by a number of dissidents beginning with Bass (1955) but including, among others, Chapman and Campbell (1957); Jackson and Messick (1957); Leavitt, Hax, and Roche (1955); and Peabody (1961). They have argued that acquiescent-response style is powerfully present in the F Scale. The primary empirical basis for this conclusion has been the frequent demonstration that "reversed" authoritarianism scales do not correlate highly negatively with the original scale. A tendency to acquiesce, regardless of the content of the items being responded to, could explain these insufficiently negative (and, on occasion, even somewhat positive) correlations.

However, the implications of these findings continue to remain obscure and certainly disputable because the empirical demonstrations all appear to have foundered on the rocky question of: *Just what constitutes a "reversal?"* As far back as Cady (1923), it was recognized that reversing complicated statements involves formidable and even unresolvable lexical difficulties. In many circumstances, rejection of an item and its opposite or endorsement of an item and its reversal—behavior which has been construed as evidence for an acquiescence effect—does not represent psychological inconsistency. For close analyses of the multifaceted problem of item reversal, the reader should consult Christie, Havel, and Seidenberg (1958); Ong (1963); and Rorer (1963). It is worth noting here, as one indication of the hazards of reversal, the finding of Mogar (1960) who correlated the Bass and the Jackson and Messick reversed F Scales. These two reversed (and presumably identical) scales correlated only a mild .35 with each other—a figure of about the same magnitude (except, of course, for sign) as the correlations obtained between the original F Scale and its various reversals.

Most recently, Rokeach (1963) on a very different tack has put forward a refreshingly simple and thus far tenable hypothesis to explain why a person may agree with a statement and also with its apparent opposite. He suggests that the reversed authoritarianism scales, by virtue of their style of phrasing and unambiguous antidemocratic content, tend to encourage lying by certain subjects who respond more faithfully to the original scales where items are expressed in a "pseudodemocratic" manner. For the present, this conjecture appears as compatible with existing evidence as does the acquiescence interpretation.

The debate on the role of acquiescence within the F and related scales continues, with no clear verdict yet in sight. Meanwhile, however, the claims for the cardinality of acquiescence have been extended to include personality inventories as similarly receptive vehicles for this response style. In pressing this view, of course, it by no means follows that an acquiescence tendency perhaps manifested in response to ambiguous, abstruse, personally peripheral statements of opinion, as are contained in authoritarianism scales, is the same as or even related to the acquiescence tendency presumed to operate in an inventory such as the MMPI, where statements have direct, intimate, and high relevance for the responder. Instead, the role of acquiescence-response style within the MMPI must be evaluated in its own right.

THE INDIRECT EVIDENCE FOR ACQUIESCENCE WITHIN THE MMPI

Two lines of evidence have been invoked in support of acquiescence-response style as an important determiner of the scores an individual achieves on MMPI scales. The first of these, now to be evaluated, takes an indirect route, seeking to show by various derivative analyses that some recurrent patterns of MMPI results are strikingly assimilable to an acquiescence interpretation or that MMPI relationships exist which are discrepant from a content-oriented point of view but concordant with the acquiescence hypothesis. Recent and already important instances of this approach are the reinterpretation of the factor structure of the MMPI based upon observation of a curious correlate of the factor loadings of MMPI scales (Messick & Jackson, 1961a) and the impressive separation of "true" and "false" MMPI subscales as revealed by factor analysis (Jackson & Messick, 1961; 1962).

The second, direct method of studying the ramifications of acquiescence we consider in the next section. This form of the empirical argument relies upon "pure" acquiescence scales and the consequent MMPI correlates of these content-free measures. One recent such measure is the *Dy-3* MMPI scale, used as a "marker variable" or criterion for acquiescence in one study (Jackson & Messick, 1961) and found to have the highest acquiescence representation in another (Jackson & Messick, 1962). The study by Couch and Keniston (1960), which has been particularly influential in advancing the cause of acquiescence, also hinges on a "pure" acquiescence measure albeit one derived outside the MMPI and only later related to it.

The Confounding of Acquiescence and Content in the Factorial Interpretation of the MMPI

The typical result of the dozen or so factor analyses of MMPI-scale intercorrelations available in the literature (and the many more not published) is the finding of two main factors and a variety of smaller, presumably less important factors.[3] The first two factor dimensions are highly reproducible from sample to sample and explain a very large percentage of the communal variance; the factors beyond the first two tend to explain small portions of the variance and to be more ephemeral, probably being functions of the particular subject sample studied.

Messick and Jackson (1961a), in a recent look at factorial studies of the MMPI noted a further consistency in the results reported. For each of eleven factor-analytic studies of MMPI scales, they correlated the factor loadings of the scales on the first factor with an index of the extent to which a scale had the potential for reflecting acquiescence. The index of acquiescence which they

---

[3] It is important to note that when the intercorrelations of MMPI *items* are factored (*e.g.*, Comrey, 1957a; 1957b; 1958a; 1958b; *et al.*) or when MMPI *subscales* are analyzed (Lingoes, 1960), a radically different factor structure emerges. There are a number of implications of this interaction between MMPI-factor structure and the micro-macro level of MMPI data being analyzed, some of which are drawn at later points in this monograph.

employed "was the proportion of items keyed true on each scale, which, assuming that the acquiescence-evoking properties of items are uniform over all MMPI scales, can be considered to reflect the extent to which total scores on a scale are influenced by consistent tendencies to respond 'true'" (Messick & Jackson, 1961a, p. 300). The correlations between factor loadings and the proportion of items keyed true were, in the Messick and Jackson study, significant in 8 of the 11 separate tests of their hypothesis that "the largest factor is interpretable in terms of acquiescence." The coefficients were often astonishingly high (4 above .85), and even in the few instances where their hypothesis was not supported, the factor structures involved could in all likelihood have been rotated to produce a much better fit to the acquiescence measure.

Such consistent support for the Messick and Jackson hypothesis, however, does not carry the necessary implication that one of the primary factors in the MMPI is *better* conceptualized as an acquiescence dimension. Certainly, an explanation must be forthcoming for the pattern of the Messick and Jackson results,[4] but their evidence for an acquiescence-response style is no more than circumstantial. Strictly, their findings demonstrate only that *a confounding of acquiescence and of content exists in the MMPI scales*, that *acquiescence is as tenable an interpretation of one primary MMPI factor as is a content interpretation*. What is required next—and before affirming a preference—is an unconfounding of acquiescence and content in MMPI scales so that these competing interpretations can run their race. Until acquiescence and content are separated and their respective contributions to MMPI-response consistency assessed, no positive claims can be made for either interpretation. Traditional MMPI users cannot ignore the possibility that acquiescence may be importantly, even decisively, involved in the test. Nor can propounders of the acquiescence viewpoint assert that content is unimportant. In the body of their paper, Messick and Jackson implicitly recognize the confounding problem by carefully and qualifiedly phrasing their argument for acquiescence as a suggested and possible alternative to an interpretation in terms of meaning. It is unfortu-

[4] See Chapter 5.

nate that in their final, summary remarks, they advance their preferred interpretation more conclusively than the logic of their analysis warrants.

Artifact and Content in the Analysis of "True" and "False" MMPI Subscales

In two recent studies, Jackson and Messick (1961; 1962) have partitioned the MMPI clinical and validity scales into subscales containing only the "true"- or only the "false"-keyed items and then factor-analyzed the intercorrelations among these subscales. They believe this design "permits a delineation of variance attributable to acquiescence within MMPI scales and allows for a more systematic appraisal of the effects of this variable than would be the case with the usual composite total scores obtained. . . ." (1962, p. 286). They were able, with three different samples, to almost completely separate "true"- and "false"-keyed subscales on their first factor after rotation. In only one instance in the three samples, does a "true" subscale have a negative loading or a "false" subscale a positive loading on the first factor, and even the solitary exception could have been eliminated by a slight rotational change. Additionally, they report that the correlations between the "true" and "false" subscales constituting an MMPI clinical scale, even when allowance is made for the attenuating effects of unreliability, are quite often low and, distressingly, even negative in certain instances. These findings are judged by Jackson and Messick to testify further for the presence of "massive response-style effects" in the MMPI.

Unfortunately, the analytical design used by Jackson and Messick—while at first glance appealing—has the bad luck to be seriously affected by the presence of item overlap among MMPI scales. Although it is well known that such item overlap exists, its extent and effect is, as a rule, not recognized. Although for some inquiries, item overlap does not affect the validity of the conclusions, in other instances, as in the Jackson and Messick design, the effect of the item overlap can be misleading.

When two scales have overlapping items scored in the same direction, their correlation of course will increase. In part, this increased correlation is valid because if two scales are independently derived, the subsequently observed item overlap testifies to an empirical relation between the two experimentally independent scale criteria. But, in usage thereafter, the overlapping items contribute, besides valid covariance, covariance that is *not* related to the dimensions these scales measure. Item overlap causes the unique variance of an item—variance that is reliable but item specific and variance that is due to error—to be treated as dimensionally meaningful variance. Because, typically, the dimensionally valid convariance of an MMPI item is quite low (average interitem correlations are of the order of only .10), the complete covariance (*i.e.*, correlations of 1.0) between numerous overlapping items can improperly boost scale intercorrelations an appreciable degree.[5]

Consider now the extent of item overlap among MMPI scales. The overlap figures to follow are based upon the eight clinical scales of the MMPI; *Hs, D, Hy, Pd, Pa, Pt, Sc,* and *Ma*.[6] These scales contain, respectively, the following number of keyed items: 33, 60, 50, 40, 48, 78, and 46—for a total of 415. The 415 keyed responses are distributed over 261 different MMPI statements, requiring that 154 (or 59%) of the keyed items be at least duplicated. Appearing in only one scale are 151 items; 74 items appear in two different scales; 30 items are used in three different scales; 4 items appear in four scales; and 2 items are keyed in five of the eight scales inspected. Of the 154 item overlaps, there are only 11

---

[5] There are several possible approaches to eliminating the artifactual influence of item overlap on the correlation between scales while recognizing the valid component of this covariance. One simple method is to calculate the correlation between the two scales with all overlapping items excluded, then adjusting the coefficient via the Spearman-Brown formula to reflect the correlation between scales of original length. Presuming item interchangeability, the adjusted coefficient estimates the correlation between the two original scales with item specific covariance removed.

[6] Calculations were restricted to these eight scales because these scales are the original and still most frequently employed MMPI scales and are the core set within the Jackson and Messick study. In addition, the job of reporting the findings remains simple so long as only pathology-relevant scales are studied. The tenor of the results based upon these eight scales does not change to a significant degree as other widely used scales are introduced (*e.g., Si, SD, Es, MAS*).

instances of scoring reversal. Of these 11 reversals, 8 involve the *Ma* scale, most often with the *D* scale. It is generally unappreciated that *where item overlap occurs in the MMPI—and it occurs often—the overlapping items are almost invariably scored in identical or equivalent directions.*

What is the effect of item overlap upon factor analyses of MMPI scales, and in particular, upon factor analyses of "true" and "false" subscales? The effect, which will be shown to be appreciable, is to inflate the correlations among MMPI scales by "locking in"—as communal variance—variation which is actually item specific but repeated in more than one scale. Item overlap, by inflating the correlations among MMPI scales, causes the first few factors subsequently extracted to "explain" more of the variance than, in fact, they do encompass. In addition, item overlap causes the derived communalities of overlapping scales to emerge appreciably higher than the reliabilities of the scales entitle them to be.

When MMPI scales are further separated into their "true" and "false" subscales, intercorrelations as a function of item overlap persist but in a newly misleading way. *Because there are so few scoring reversals when item overlap occurs, the correlation component due to overlap covariance now exists primarily among like keyed subscales.* Thus, the intercorrelations among "true" subscales or among "false" subscales are raised unfairly by the presence of item overlap. However, the correlations between appropriately paired "true" and "false" subscales are not so affected. The clustering—based on item overlap—of the "true" subscales and of the "false" subscales has obvious implications for the factor structure later found.

To exemplify the prior reasoning and to evaluate the extent to which item overlap has affected some of the conclusions drawn about the MMPI, the intercorrelations of "true" and "false" subscales solely on the basis of item overlap were calculated, using the well-known formula for correlation as a function of the number of common elements (*cf.*, McNemar, 1962, p. 133). The "true" and "false" subscales studied are taken from the eight clinical MMPI scales. The resulting 16 x 16 correlation matrix may be seen in Table 1. A clear clustering is visually apparent and many

TABLE 1
Intercorrelations of MMPI "True" and "False" Subscales as a Function of Item Overlap

	Hs_t	D_t	Hy_t	Pd_t	Pa_t	Pt_t	Sc_t	Ma_t	Hs_f	D_f	Hy_f	Pd_f	Pa_f	Pt_f	Sc_f	Ma_f
Hs_t	25	—	—	—	—	—	—	—	—	—	—	—	—	—	—	—
D_t	20	29	—	—	—	—	—	—	—	—	—	—	—	—	—	—
Hy_t	25	25	25	—	—	—	—	—	—	—	—	—	—	—	—	—
Pd_t	00	09	06	24	—	—	—	—	—	—	—	—	—	—	—	—
Pa_t	00	05	00	24	31	—	—	—	—	—	—	—	—	—	—	—
Pt_t	05	29	22	16	13	31	—	—	—	—	—	—	—	—	—	—
Sc_t	04	20	18	19	31	31	31	—	—	—	—	—	—	—	—	—
Ma_t	00	04	05	07	10	08	22	22	—	—	—	—	—	—	—	—
Hs_f	00	−05	00	00	00	00	00	00	47	—	—	—	—	—	—	—
D_f	00	00	00	00	00	00	−02	−11	20	26	—	—	—	—	—	—
Hy_f	00	00	00	00	00	00	00	−05	47	21	47	—	—	—	—	—
Pd_f	00	00	00	00	00	00	00	−03	04	16	26	26	—	—	—	—
Pa_f	00	00	00	00	00	00	00	−09	06	04	15	10	15	—	—	—
Pt_f	00	00	00	00	00	00	00	00	07	26	10	07	00	26	—	—
Sc_f	00	00	00	00	00	00	00	00	15	07	10	14	07	15	15	—
Ma_f	00	00	00	00	00	00	00	00	00	00	13	18	08	00	07	18

of the correlations are high enough to command—if we did not know their basis—interpretive attention.

This correlation matrix was then factor-analyzed by means of the centroid method, using as the initial communality estimate for a subscale the highest correlation of that subscale with another. Two factors, of course, extract all variance in this totally constrained situation and are reported, in unrotated form, in Table 2. It will be observed there that the perfect factor separation of "true" and "false" subscales emphasized by Jackson and Messick

TABLE 2

Unrotated Factor Matrix Underlying Overlap-Based MMPI Correlations

	1	2	h^2
Hs_t	162	186	0.61
D_t	340	321	.219
Hy_t	258	298	.155
Pd_t	221	248	.110
Pa_t	233	269	.127
Pt_t	326	366	.240
Sc_t	401	411	.330
Ma_t	230	118	.067
Hs_f	−358	333	.239
D_f	−321	257	.169
Hy_f	−477	435	.417
Pd_f	−287	279	.160
Pa_f	−171	132	.047
Pt_f	−221	215	.095
Sc_f	−219	213	.093
Ma_f	−160	151	.048

as evidence for acquiescence is found as well in our artifact-evaluating analysis—and that all the "true" subscales have positive loadings on our Factor 1 and all the "false" subscales have negative loadings on this factor. Moreover, many of the factor loadings are large enough to warrant—in another context—respectful interpretation.

It would appear then, that the factor structures obtained by Jackson and Messick in their analyses of "true" and "false" MMPI subscales are susceptible to an alternative interpretation and do not speak compellingly for the acquiescence interpretation so long as the potent and permeating influence of item overlap resides in their design.

Another simpler and more direct finding of Jackson and Messick presents, if not positive evidence for acquiescence, perhaps inferential support of their view. This is their observation that the correlations between the "true" and "false" portions of MMPI scales are disappointingly low and even reversed in certain instances. Clearly, the notion of acquiescence *could* provide a sufficient explanation of these data. However, again, closer analysis blurs the conclusiveness of any interpretation.

To begin, it must be noted that the situation is not quite so bad as their analysis suggests. Quite properly, they recognized the attenuating effects of unreliability upon their correlations and adjusted for this effect. Unfortunately, their correction was in partial error.

In order to correct for the limiting effects of unreliability, estimates of the reliabilities of the subscales are required. Jackson and Messick employed as their estimates either the Kuder-Richardson Formula 21 reliability of a subscale or its communality within their factor analysis, *whichever was higher*. Almost invariably, they used the communality estimate. Their reasoning was that Kuder-Richardson reliabilities underestimate somewhat the stability of measures while communality in factor theory is always less than but may approach the true reliability of a measure. Accordingly, the calculated communalities should, if higher than the understating Kuder-Richardson figures, be employed as the better reliability estimate because they are higher lower bounds.

However, this rationale fails to recognize the effect of item overlap in their factor analysis which, as we have shown, inappropriately raises calculated communalities. Since the correction for unreliability is small when the reliability estimates used are high, the usage by Jackson and Messick of overstatements of the reliability does not fully adjust for this perturbation. When due allowance is made, by subtraction from their communality figures, for the communal variance unfairly introduced by item overlap, the picture changes.

Restricting recomputation again to the eight clinical scales of the MMPI, we find that the "true" and "false" portions of the *Hs, Pt,* and *Sc* scales correlate to the limit set by their reliabilities and thus may be said to be content-representing. The "true" and "false" components of the remaining five scales are not conceptually equivalent judging from the three Jackson and Messick samples. It is only with respect to these latter scales that the question may be asked: Are these discrepancies ascribable to the canceling influence of acquiescence? Or, may these nominally equivalent but differently functioning subscales be viewed instead as measuring psychologically different dimensions?

The question is a large one, calling for complicated analyses beyond the interests of this monograph. It may even be an unfair statement of the problem since the failure of equivalence between "true" and "false" portions of certain MMPI scales when applied to psychologically heterogeneous (or differently homogeneous) subject samples does not mean that when these scales are employed with samples comparable to the original standardization samples, the subscales will again prove noncomparable. The empirical method of scale construction used in evolving the clinical scales of the MMPI required that all keyed items be criterion-relevant. The relationships among the items defining a scale can well change when noncomparable samples are studied, as has been the case subsequently. As a rule, psychologists have been slow to recognize that the pattern of correlations among personality variables (items) is often a reliable function of the specific subject population being sampled.

For the moment, our line of argument is to show that the failure of full equivalence between the "true" and "false" portions of certain MMPI scales can as well be construed in contentual terms as via the notion of acquiescence. In so doing, we rely heavily on earlier demonstrations that various of the clinical scales of the MMPI have, when applied to clinically heterogeneous samples, poor internal consistency properties and that when psychologically homogeneous subscales are developed, an imbalance of keying may exist in the newly partitioned scales. The reader interested in details may consult the work of Harris and Lingoes (1955), Little and Fisher (1958), and the series of papers by Comrey (1957a; 1957b; 1957c; 1958a; 1958b; 1958c; 1958d; 1958e).

To exemplify our point, consider the *Pa* scale of the MMPI which contains 25 items keyed "true" and 15 items keyed "false." The "true" and "false" *Pa* subscales correlated appreciably negatively in all three of the samples studied by Jackson and Messick (unadjusted correlations of —.30, —.35, and —.27)—the worst performance of any of the MMPI scales. But what kind of items typify the "true" *Pa* subscale? And what kind of items typify the "false" *Pa* subscale? Fortunately, an independent assessment of the item content of the *Pa* scale exists because some years ago and preceding the advent of the acquiescence interpretation, Harris and Lingoes (1955) constructed three subscales within the *Pa* scale in order to aid in the interpretation of MMPI profiles.

On strictly psychological grounds, they divided the *Pa* scale into subscales labeled *Pa 1:* Ideas of external influence (17 items, 16 being keyed "true"); *Pa 2:* Poignancy (9 items, 7 being keyed "true"); and *Pa 3:* Moral virtue (10 items, 9 being keyed "false").

Typical items in the *Pa 1* subscale are the following:

123. I believe I am being followed (true).
293. Someone has been trying to influence my mind (true).
364. People say insulting and vulgar things about me (true).

Items in the *Pa 2* subscale include:

24. No one seems to understand me (true).
299. I think I feel more intensely than most people do (true).
341. At times I hear so well it bothers me (true).

Some of the items defining the *Pa 3* subscale are:

93. I think most people would lie to get ahead (false).
124. Most people will use somewhat unfair means to gain profit or an advantage rather than to lose it (false).
313. The man who provides temptation by leaving valuable unprotected property is about as much to blame for its theft as the one who steals it (false).

It is clear by inspection that the content of *Pa 1* is very different psychologically from the content of *Pa 3*. Similarly, the content of *Pa 2* is very different from the content of *Pa 3*. In their normative work, Harris and Lingoes report negative correlations of about —.3 between *Pa 3* and *Pa 1* or *Pa 2* and moderately sized positive correlations between *Pa 1* and *Pa 2*. This pattern of interrelationships among the *Pa* subscales was found again by Lingoes (1960) in studies of four additional samples.

Now, by virtue of the part-whole relationship between the "true" *Pa* subscale and the *Pa 1* and *Pa 2* subscales and between the "false" *Pa* subscale and *Pa 3*, the Harris and Lingoes findings can subsume the negative correlation found by Jackson and Messick between the "true" and "false" *Pa* subscales. Again a confounding exists. Although response imbalance is also present in the Harris scales, the presence as well of indisputable content homogeneities leaves the interpretation of the basis of these results up in the air. Acquiescence could explain the results, but for the present a preference for a contentual interpretation is also supportable—differences between the "true" and "false" *Pa* subscales could be expected in nonparanoid samples because of content differences between the two subscales.

The above argument with respect to the *Pa* scale can be applied as well to the other MMPI scales which fail to manifest sufficient correlation between their "true" and "false" portions. Content differences between the "true" and "false" subscales can be argued as present, and thus confounding again denies us a clarity of conclusion.

Finally, in regard to the sometimes insufficiently high correlation between the "true" and "false" portions of an MMPI scale, we note an often unrecognized psychometric constraint on the values a Pearson product-moment coefficient can take. It is widely but mistakenly believed that the possible range of Pearson correlations is always from a plus to minus one. In fact, these limits apply if, and only if, the two distributions being related are of identical shape; otherwise, the theoretical bounds move closer—sometimes, appreciably closer—to zero. The limitation on the maximum size of phi coefficients as a function of disparity of marginal splits is well known; exactly the same limitation applies to Pearson correlations derived from disparate continuous distributions (Carroll, 1961).

Applying this recognition to the MMPI, the theoretically maximum correlations between "true" and "false" subscales were calculated for the nine clinical scales of the inventory, on each of nine different samples. On the average, over all scales and over all samples, 10% of the presumed variance is lost because of differences between the score distributions generated by the "true" and "false" portions of a scale. For some scales, the drop from unity is small (*e.g., Si, Pt, D*); for others, the maximum correlation obtainable, given the shapes of the respective "true" and "false" score distributions, is lowered appreciably (*e.g., Hy, Pa, Hs*). Thus, this limitation on Pearson coefficients rather than acquiescence underlies to a significant degree the failure of certain "true" and "false" MMPI subscales to correlate perfectly. On its own, range restriction is insufficient as a full explanation of the incongruence between "true" and "false" subscales. But given the proportions of variance usually explained in psychology, it is apparent that the operation of this psychometric constraint contributes substantially to the presumed evidence for acquiescence in the form of less-than-unity correlations between "true" and "false" subscales.[7]

Constructing Content-Free Measures of Acquiescence

Developing a measure of content-free acquiescence within the MMPI does not admit of an easy solution. Various rationales have been employed but still true is Jackson and Messick's (1958) observation of several years ago that good measuring devices for acquiescence do not exist. Studies by Foster (1961), Foster and

---

[7] It is worth mentioning, before leaving this section, some recent indirect evidence *against* acquiescence. Using the research design of constructing "reversed" scales, Rorer (1963) has been able to develop reversed scales which correlate highly negatively with the original MMPI scales. Ong (1963), using personality-relevant items but not the MMPI, has also reported successfully reversed scales. Prior to construction of their respective reversed items, both of these researchers most carefully analyzed the problem of item reversal. Although failure of reversed scales to be sufficiently diametrical can be explained away as not necessarily due to acquiescence, the accomplishment of successful reversals leaves little logical possibility for the acquiescence interpretation.

Grigg (1963), McGee (1962), and Siller and Chipman (1963) all report disappointingly low correlations among various proposed acquiescence measures or correlations explainable in alternative terms. Why is this so? Why has development of an acceptable acquiescence measure taken so long and still not met with success?

We have already noted the equivocal character, as an index of acquiescence, of the proportion of responses keyed "true." Another measure which has been employed is the Deviant True score (a simple count of the items answered "true" by a subject which typically are answered "false" by normal criterion groups) and its apparent opposite, the Deviant False score (a count of the items answered "false" by a subject which typically are answered "true" by normal criterion groups). Barnes (1956a) has observed the collinearity of the Deviant True score with the first factor of the MMPI and the strong relationship of the Deviant False score with the second MMPI factor. Messick and Jackson (1961a, p. 302) suggest that, in effect, the scales developed by Welsh (1956) to measure the first two factors in the MMPI, scales Welsh christened A (for "anxiety") and R (for "repression"), are tantamount to short forms of the Deviant True and Deviant False scales since 38 of the 39 items in the A scale are keyed true and all 40 of the items in the R scale are keyed false.

Our previous point—of a confounding between meaning and acquiescence—obviously applies to any would-be interpretation of these pairs of scales. Further complicating the status of these pairs of scales as converse measures of acquiescence is the fact that they are orthogonally 'rather than diametrically related. Deviant True and Deviant False scales are, in general, uncorrelated, as found by Barnes (1956b), Wiggins (1962), and the present writer.[8] A and R are essentially orthogonal in a variety of studies, also.[9] Although Messick and Jackson acknowledge that these results cannot be encompassed by a response set of generalized acquiescence, they believe:

[8] In the Samples A through E analyzed for the purposes of this monograph, the correlations between the Deviant True and Deviant False scales were —.16, .07, .51, —.15, and .30, respectively.

[9] In the five samples, A through E, the correlations between the A and R scales were —.24, —.01, .00, —.31, and —.24, respectively.

It is not necessary to postulate two independent sets to agree and to disagree. . . . All that is required to account for the findings is the operation of at least one other factor in conjunction with acquiescence. Thus, the A scale can have a high positive loading on an acquiescence factor and the R scale a high negative loading, yet the two scales could be uncorrelated if they *both* (italics added) had positive, or negative loadings on some other dimension. . . . A particularly likely candidate for such a role is the stylistic tendency to respond in a desirable way (Messick & Jackson, 1961a, p. 302).

Although Messick and Jackson place much emphasis upon this conjectural possibility, they have not examined it empirically. In order to reconcile the anomalous (for the acquiescence interpretation) situation of approximate orthogonality between A and R scales, *both* of these scales must be high on social desirability (SD) or *both* must be low. This implication can be evaluated directly by reference to an earlier observation reported by Wiggins and Rumrill (1959). Wiggins and Rumrill scaled the MMPI with respect to the social desirability continuum and found that the mean SD scale value for items in the A scale is significantly different ($p < .001$) from the mean SD value for items in the R scale. The items in the A scale tend to be socially undesirable, the items in the R scale tend to be neutral or intermediate with respect to social desirability. Clearly then, social desirability as the second primary factor within the MMPI cannot be invoked to explain away the orthogonality of A and R, and no other factor in these factor analyses is sizable enough to interact importantly with an acquiescence dimension as Messick and Jackson would require. It must be concluded, therefore, that the relations between the A and R (and between Deviant True and Deviant False) scales cannot be subsumed under the rubric of acquiescence-response set.[10]

[10] As an alternative way of evaluating the viability of the Messick and Jackson conjecture, it should be noted again that the A and Deviant True scales are collinear with the social (un)desirability dimension. The correlations between Edwards' SD scale (1957) and Welsh's A scale consistently are at the limits set by their respective reliabilities. In the present study, for example, the correlations between SD and A are $-.87$, $-.91$, $-.92$, $-.82$, and $-.92$ for the five samples analyzed. The same equivalence relationship obtains between the SD and Deviant True scale. Within the present samples, the correlations between SD and Deviant True are $-.77$, $-.74$, $-.87$, $-.80$,

Wiggins (1962) has recently summarized various other efforts to construct pure measures of acquiescence and has noted some of the difficulties and failures attending such efforts. The inevitable, intrinsic paradox besetting research on acquiescence is that, as Wiggins remarks:

The agreement tendency has been defined with respect to *heterogeneous* and ambiguous items in such a manner that internal consistency in a presumed measure of acquiescence may itself be interpreted as content variance which would vitiate the acquiescence measure on logical grounds (Wiggins, 1962, p. 235).

Yet, unless reliability of the acquiescence measure is established, the significance of a generalized tendency to acquiescence is questionable. Although it is possible, as we will see, to formulate MMPI measures which unequivocally reflect content while excluding acquiescence, it is not possible to construct a measure of acquiescence wherein, *a priori*, content considerations are guaranteed to be uninvolved.

Resolution of this complication requires—instead of contention or unawareness—an explicit confrontation of the possibility of a core of meaning in the formally defined acquiescence measure. Assertions that the items defining an acquiescence scale "make no psychological sense" (Couch & Keniston, 1960) may be correct, but they may also be naïve. MMPI acquiescence measures proposed as "pure" indices must be examined empirically and closely to test their underlying presumption that the items employed are psychologically heterogeneous. Thus, acquiescence scales constructed by selecting items of high controversiality (items which result in splits of approximately 50-50 in a normal population) (Fricke, 1957) have been found to be loaded with a social undesirability component (Hanley, 1961). Acquiescence scales constructed simply by keying "true" a large number of presumably heterogeneous items (Cohn, 1952; Couch & Keninston, 1960)

and —.88, again at about the attainable limits. Correlations of this magnitude indicate all the variance in the A or Deviant True scale can be "understood" in terms of a social desirability dimension. Accordingly, *no additional variance remains within these measures to be explained.* There is no psychometric room to invoke an acquiescence interpretation unless it is argued that Edwards' SD scale is not a sufficient defining measure of the social-desirability dimension.

have been found on closer analysis to also reflect social undesirability (Gage, Leavitt & Stone, 1957; Edwards & Walker, 1961a).

The Jackson and Messick Dy-3 Scale
as a Content-Free Acquiescence Measure

Recently, and as another aspect of their analysis of "true" and "false" MMPI subscales, Jackson and Messick (1961; 1962) have used as an acquiescence measure a set of keyed "true" items, labeled the *Dy-3* scale, which are in the middle range of the social desirability continuum. In their first factor analysis, Jackson and Messick employed the *Dy-3* scale as a marker or criterion variable through which they positioned a factor dimension of the MMPI they interpreted as acquiescence. In two later analyses, although not employed as a criterion, the *Dy-3* scale had the highest loadings on the factor labeled acquiescence. Because of the centrality of the *Dy-3* scale to the Jackson and Messick analyses, and because of its appreciable reliability (Jackson and Messick report K-R Formula 21 reliabilities of the *Dy-3* scale in three samples of .75, .74, and .58; the K-R Formula 20 reliabilities of the *Dy-3* scale within the five samples studied for the present monograph are .75, .68, .40, .72, and .71), it seemed highly pertinent to examine the internal structure of the *Dy-3* scale.

Accordingly, the 59 MMPI items defining the *Dy-3* scale [11] were factor-analyzed, the data being derived from the MMPI protocols of a sample of 100 military officers. Phi coefficients were employed as the index of correlation in the light of the recent study by Comrey and Levonian (1958) of several measures of item association. The principal axis method of factor analysis was used, with initial item communalities estimated by the highest interitem correlation of each item. For the purposes of the present inquiry, the factors found were *not* rotated in order to preclude preferential location of the reference axis. However, it

---

[11] The *Dy-3* scale, as originally constructed, included 60 items. In kindly providing the scoring key for the *Dy-3* scale, Dr. Messick noted that one of the items listed was in apparent error in that it did not meet the criterion of social neutrality set for including items in the scale. This item was eliminated from our analyses, a change so minor it can be disregarded.

should be mentioned that a varimax rotation of the obtained factors does not change appreciably the initial factor pattern.

What kind of factor structure within an inventory scale comports with an acquiescence interpretation? Two possibilities can be reasoned. The first schema requires that only one factor be present, the factor loadings of the items being both small and equal. An alternative factor structure supporting an acquiescence interpretation of a scale requires the presence of a large (how many is large?) number of only slightly oblique factors, each factor extracting an equal and consequently small amount of the total variance. Only one second-order factor should underlie this first-order factor structure if an acquiescence dimension is to be inferred. A concomitant requirement, in either case, is that the acquiescence items (or the many first-order factor scales) be submitted to a set of independent judges for interpretive specification of the basic contentual dimension underlying the items (or first-order factors). These judges should manifest only casual agreement in their interpretations if the role of content is to be excluded.

In point of fact, the results obtained from the factor analysis of the *Dy-3* items cannot be fitted to either of the required factor structures. First of all, in a matrix which by the acquiescence hypothesis should have a generally positive manifold, one-third of the phi coefficients (33.8%) are negative. Only the first three factors extract large and interpretable portions of the variance while the remaining factors encompass little variance and are insufficiently defined. Thus, neither of the acquiescence-supporting factor structures underlies the *Dy-3* scale. Nineteen *Dy-3* items have factor loadings of at least .30 on the first factor, nine items have loadings of this magnitude on the second factor, and nine *Dy-3* items meet this criterion with respect to the third factor. From the fourth factor on, no factor is defined by more than four items and usually only one or two items have prominent loadings.

The items defining the first three factors may be read from Table 3. The first factor has all but one item answered in the "true" direction and therefore, if considered out of the present context, this factor might be viewed as an acquiescence measure. However, the contentual homogeneity of these items points with

TABLE 3

The *Dy-3* Items Defining the First Three Factors Found Within the *Dy-3* Acquiescence Measure

MMPI Item No.	Keyed Response	
Dy-3 Factor 1		
30	Y	At times I feel like swearing.
71	Y	I think a great many people exaggerate their misfortune in order to gain the sympathy and help of others.
92	Y	I would like to be a nurse.
105	Y	Sometimes when I am not feeling well I am cross.
135	Y	If I could get into a movie without paying and be sure I was not seen I would probably do it.
165	Y	I like to know some important people because it makes me feel important.
208	Y	I like to flirt.
327	Y	My mother or father often made me obey even when I thought that it was unreasonable.
390	Y	I have often felt badly over being misunderstood when trying to keep someone from making a mistake.
402	Y	I often must sleep over a matter before I decide what to do.
404	Y	People have often misunderstood my intentions when I was trying to put them right and be helpful.
410	Y	I would certainly enjoy beating a crook at his own game.
425	Y	I dream frequently.
436	Y	People generally demand more respect for their own rights than they are willing to allow for others.
465	Y	I have several times had a change of heart about my life work.

27

TABLE 3 *(Continued)*

MMPI Item No.	Keyed Response	
505	Y	I have had periods when I felt so full of pep that sleep did not seem necessary for days at a time.
536	Y	It makes me angry to have people hurry me.
566	Y	I like movie love scenes.
548	N	I never attend a sexy show if I can avoid it.

Dy-3 Factor 2

33	Y	I have had very peculiar and strange experiences.
206	Y	I am very religious (more than most people).
232	Y	I have been inspired to a program of life based on duty which I have since carefully followed.
373	Y	I feel sure that there is only one true religion.
490	Y	I read in the Bible several times a week.
548	Y	I never attend a sexy show if I can avoid it.
550	Y	I like repairing a door latch.
195	N	I do not like everyone I know.
500	N	I readily become one hundred percent sold on a good idea.

Dy-3 Factor 3

6	Y	I like to read newspaper articles on crime.
434	Y	I would like to be an auto racer.
435	Y	Usually I would prefer to work with women.
550	Y	I like repairing a door latch.
120	N	My table manners are not quite as good at home as when I am out in company.
206	N	I am very religious (more than most people).
225	N	I gossip a little at times.
373	N	I feel sure that there is only one true religion.
402	N	I often must sleep over a matter before I decide what to do.

equal plausibility to an interpretation of this factor as a measure of the general tendency to be an under-controller—to express impulse directly, to be candid in acknowledging the desirous and aggressive feelings that in fact beset all people, and to be volatile and expansive. There are strong elements of character deficiency in the kind of under-control portrayed by these items—the qualities of restlessness, cynicism, self-centeredness, and hypersensitivity. But we suggest these characteristics appear to overlay rather than to displace from primacy the impulse-control dimension. This factor has been found before—in purer form—in other factor analyses of the MMPI, and later in this monograph we shall encounter it again.[12]

Of the nine items defining the second factor, seven are answered in the "true" direction. These items, by their content, imply a character structure which is at once fundamentalist and constricted. Spontaneity is eschewed and it would appear that religion provides the prop by which personal control is maintained.

The nine items by which the third *Dy-3* factor is specified include four answered in the "true" direction. The personality implications of the content of this item set are not so clear nor are they cleanly separable from those of the first two factors. It appears that the underlying dimension at one end partakes of the under-control reflected by the first factor while the other end of the continuum shares similarity with the fundamentalism portrayed by the second factor. A more satisfactory rationale for this factor dimension must await a more extensive set of defining items.

---

[12] To buttress the preceding interpretation, two MMPI-experienced psychologists were asked to read the items defining this factor and to indicate, from a list of 70 personality-descriptive adjectives (Block, 1961), the 10 adjectives most succinctly portraying the kind of person who would score high on the *Dy-3 Factor 1* scale. In contemplating the contentual significance of these items, the judges had no idea of the source of this scale. For the one judge, the 10 most salient adjectives were *changeable, easily hurt, frank, guileful, impulsive, rebellious, restless, sarcastic, self-indulgent,* and *tactless.* The second judge evaluated the person scoring high on the *Dy-3 Factor 1* scale as *assertive, changeable, energetic, frank, impulsive, introspective, rebellious, resentful, sarcastic,* and *unconventional.* Clearly, there is appreciable agreement in the proposed interpretations, and the formulations agree with that presented in the text.

As a means of evaluating the relative importance of these three factors within the *Dy-3* scale, the 100 MMPI protocols were scored on the three factor-scale and these scores were then correlated with each other and with the full *Dy-3* scale scores. These intercorrelations and the scale reliabilities are reported in Table 4. It should be noted that the correlations of factor scales 1 and 2 with the full *Dy-3* scale are part-whole correlations. The third factor-scale, by virtue of having about as many items keyed "false" as are keyed "true," has almost no built-in relationship with the full *Dy-3* scale.

TABLE 4
Intercorrelations of *Dy-3* with Its Factor Scales

	Dy-3	*Factor 1*	*Factor 2*	*Factor 3*
Dy-3 (Full Scale)	.75 *			
Dy-3 Factor 1	.86	.80		
Dy-3 Factor 2	.16	−.10	.52	
Dy-3 Factor 3	−.01	−.11	−.16	.46

* Entries in main diagonal are the K-R Formula 20 reliabilities of each scale.

Inspecting these correlations, it may be seen that the first factor within the *Dy-3* scale is a highly reliable measure which predicts the full *Dy-3* score almost perfectly. The first factor correlates appreciably higher with the full *Dy-3* scale than its part-whole overlap requires, a finding suggesting a component beyond the presumably present acquiescence is operating. Although seven-ninths of the items in the second factor-scale are scored in the acquiescent direction, the second factor correlates *less well* with the total score than its part-whole commonality would entail. The reason why it correlates lower than it should with the full *Dy-3* scale can again be attributed to a contentual core, this time one operating to negate the possibly operating acquiescence effect. The third factor-scale in which acquiescence is essentially absent and which can be interpreted psychologically only with great uneasiness, shows no relationship to the full *Dy-3* scale and may safely be neglected.

In summary, then, an analysis of the internal structure of the *Dy-3* scale has shown that although the *Dy-3* scale was constructed with no reference to content homogeneity, a clear and pervasive content component appears to reside within the scale. The finding of a dominant content dimension which predicts the total *Dy-3* score so well severely constrains an interpretation of the *Dy-3* scale solely as an index of acquiescence.[13] A reason why a content component emerges strongly even though a mechanical rule was employed in constituting the scale will be suggested later.

The Couch and Keniston Acquiescence Measure and
Its Content-Homogeneity

Finally, we consider more closely the ambitious study by Couch and Keniston (1960) to which we have already alluded. Strictly speaking, the acquiescence measure developed by these investigators does not come from the MMPI and so is out of our purview. However, Couch and Keniston use an item pool not unlike that of the MMPI and also relate their measure to separately obtained MMPI scores. On the basis of extensive analyses, they have concluded that their "integrated study . . . has demonstrated both the far-reaching importance of response set in the area of psychological tests and the major proposition that the agreeing response tendency is based on a central personality syn-

[13] A related and perhaps sounder proposal for the construction of an unequivocal measure of acquiescence comes from Wiggins (1962). He selected from the MMPI items which are both controversial *and* neutral with respect to social desirability on the intuitively sound grounds that consistent responses of "true" to such items would betoken an acquiescence tendency. Only a few items (27) meet this dual criterion, however, and even with this carefully selected set of items (Wiggins' *Rb* scale) the plaguing possibility of a dominating content component cannot be excluded *a priori*. Perusal of the items defining the *Rb* scale suggests, at least to this writer, that the scale contains a hard core of statements reflective of a dominant, emotionally uninhibited individual. It may not be necessary to evaluate this scale more objectively by means of factor analysis since the reliability of the *Rb* scale is so low as to suggest no stable style of responding is present. Wiggins reports a K-R Formula 21 reliability of .36 for the *Rb* scale; in the five samples studied here, the K-R Formula 20 reliabilities of the *Rb* scale were .37, .23, −.09, .41, and .22.

drome" (Couch & Keniston, 1960, p. 173). Given the intention and the theme of the present section of this monograph and the frequency with which their paper is cited, an evaluation of the Couch and Keniston contribution is in order.

Couch and Keniston begin with an intuitively appealing rationale for a pure measure of acquiescence. They specify three criteria which an appropriate measure of acquiescence should fulfill:

(a) the items should measure heterogeneous content variables from widely different psychological areas; (b) these content variables should be selected so that the total set is psychologically 'balanced' to insure an overall diffuseness of content; and (c) the total number of individual items in the overall response measure should be very large (at least 300) so that the general response tendency has sufficient opportunity to manifest itself by permeating the answer pattern in a consistent way (Couch & Keniston, 1960, p. 152).

In implementing these criteria, Couch and Keniston administered a pool of 681 personality inventory items to a sample of 61 paid volunteer male college students. These items included many (but apparently not all) of the items contained in a variety of published inventory scales plus an unspecified but large number of items written for the occasion or carried over from previous unpublished analyses. From this generally unavailable pool of items, 360 items were selected to represent 30 different bipolar psychological dimensions. For each of these dimensions, an equal (but unspecified) number of items on "opposite" ends of the continuum were included. Couch and Keniston define the number of "true" responses to these 360 items as their Overall Agreement Score (OAS) and consider this score to be a pure measure of agreeing response set. Within their sample, the split-half reliability of the OAS was .85.

Several objections can be raised against this measure and the way it was constructed. In part, these reservations stem from a failure on the part of Couch and Keniston to report many highly pertinent features of their design.

First, they mention only four of the thirty content variables included within the OAS scale. Without knowledge of the psychological dimensions contained within the OAS scale *and their empirical intercorrelations*, it remains an article of faith to assume that a "diffuseness" of content has resulted. Required instead is assuring evidence that psychological heterogeneity has been achieved.

Second, although the idea of canceling out the effect of content by including compensating items is a worthy one, it is not at all clear that any basis other than informal judgment was employed to decide upon the "oppositeness" of items. The nature of language is such that meaningful conversity is not readily obtained—and may not be presumed—as sustained efforts to reverse the Authoritarianism *F* scale testify (*cf.*, Christie, Havel, & Seidenberg, 1958; Rorer, 1963).

Third, the average interitem correlation within the 360-item acquiescence scale of Couch and Keniston can be estimated to be .0155 (by reversing the Spearman-Brown prophecy formula, knowing the reliability of the total score and the number of contributing items). This is an astonishingly low interitem correlation, being three to ten times lower than the average interitem correlation of MMPI scales based upon external psychological criteria. Although from an acquiescence-favoring point of view this state of affairs would seem to be a congenial one, for it suggests the small but steady and cumulative effect of acquiescence, it is necessary in addition to know that items are contributing approximately equally to the OAS. With so many items in this acquiescence scale and with so low an average item intercorrelation, the psychometric situation is amorphous. It could well be the case, for example, that a substantial number and even most of the items contributing toward the OAS have zero covariance but appreciable reliability of the OAS is attained because of the existence and consequent dominance within the scale of a small, psychologically homogeneous subset of items. Clearly, a factor analysis of the items upon which the OAS is based is required to quell or to evaluate this vitiating possibility.

In the meanwhile, however, it should not be thought that the suggestion of a strong content component within the Couch and Keniston acquiescence measure is idly or obfuscatingly offered. Table 5 reproduces, from Table 8 in the Couch and Keniston, 1960 paper, the 15 individual items correlating most highly with the OAS. These 15 items Couch and Keniston consider to be the best short form of the agreeing response tendency. These 15 items alone, if they have intercorrelations of the order of their impressive correlations with the total OAS, are sufficient to provide the high reliability observed in the OAS.

Unfortunately for an exclusive acquiescence interpretation, from the content of these items there emerges, without difficulty, a cohesive personality picture. A person who affirms this set of statements would appear to be one who readily expresses his de-

TABLE 5

The 15 Couch and Keniston Items Correlating Most Highly with Their Overall Agreement Score

	Correlation with OAS (N = 61)
1. Novelty has a great appeal to me.	.54
2. I crave excitement.	.54
3. It's a wonderful feeling to sit surrounded by your possessions.	.51
4. There are few things more satisfying than really to splurge on something—books, clothes, furniture, etc.	.48
5. Only the desire to achieve great things will bring a man's mind into full activity.	.47
6. Nothing is worse than an offensive odor.	.46
7. In most conversations, I tend to bounce from topic to topic.	.45
8. I really envy the man who can walk up to anybody and tell him off to his face.	.44
9. I could really shock people if I said all of the dirty things I think.	.44
10. There are few more miserable experiences than going to bed night after night knowing you are so upset that worry will not let you sleep.	.42
11. I tend to make decisions on the spur of the moment.	.42
12. Little things upset me.	.41
13. Drop reminders of yourself wherever you go and your life's trail will be well remembered.	.41
14. I like nothing better than having breakfast in bed.	.40
15. My mood is easily influenced by the people around me.	.40

sires and aggressiveness, a person who is impulsive and self-indulging, fitful and readily bored. Surprisingly, there is an impressive similarity between the kind of individual represented by these "best" OAS items and the kind of personality reflected by the first factor-scale within the *Dy-3* scale of Messick and Jackson. Again, we see an acquiescence measure that equally well may be interpreted as a measure of manifestations of undercontrol. Without knowing the historical circumstances under which the 360 items defining the OAS were aggregated, it is impossible to suggest just how this personality dimension came to confound this proposed acquiescence measure.

Because of this confounding of content and style in their measure of acquiescence, the subsequent clinical findings by Couch and Keniston that "yea-sayers" are impulsive and "nay-sayers" are inhibited has equivocal import. It may be looked upon as a theoretically significant and important-to-understand correlate or determinant of acquiescence, as Couch and Keniston would prefer. Or, alternatively, the finding that individuals who acknowledge impulsive behaviors when responding to a personality inventory are in fact impulsive may be looked upon as a partial validation of the inventory approach to personality measurement. While the dimensions of acquiescence-response set and of impulse control remain fundamentally linked, as they are in the Couch and Keniston study, it would seem these authors are not yet entitled to their conclusions.

We conclude, therefore, from this review that *all* demonstrations thus far of the role of acquiescence in the MMPI have used measures or indices of acquiescence open to the countering criticism of a confounding with content in either obvious or subtle ways. Because criteria of unequivocality have not been met, the issue is still moot. Until the significance of an acquiescence tendency clearly has been manifested in MMPI-like personality inventories, it is premature to turn, as Messick and Jackson (1961) and Couch and Keniston (1960) suggest, to consideration of the personological significance of this response style.

3

CONSTRUCTING ACQUIESCENCE-FREE MMPI SCALES

For many of the MMPI scales, the scale-defining items are keyed predominantly "true" or predominantly "false." It has been argued that an extreme score on a scale keyed one-sidedly could as well arise from a blanket tendency to acquiesce to (or to deny) all items as from a reaction to the content of the items involved. Reciprocally, we have maintained that no MMPI index of "pure" acquiescence yet proposed has been shown to be free of the confounding influence of content. As noted earlier, the requirement of reliability for an acquiescence measure inevitably develops the possibility of a content-based alternative explanation of the index. Is it possible, however, to construct content-oriented MMPI scales which indisputably or sufficiently eliminate the presence of an acquiescence component, thus permitting the scores an individual attains to be unambiguously interpretable? We suggest there is a quick and easy technique, not new, but infrequently employed, which can be applied—even retroactively—to the MMPI to exclude the influence of acquiescence.

This simple way of preventing acquiescence-response set from affecting the scores an individual earns on a scale is to insure that half of the scale-defining items are scored for the answer "true" and half for the answer "false." "Balanced scales should serve to cancel out any contamination due to agreeing response set" (Couch and Keniston, 1960, p. 156), and therefore the individual differences, correlates, and factor structure of such balanced scales can be interpreted without recourse to an acquiescence component. It is likely, as one beneficial consequence of the con-

36

cern raised about acquiescence, that future inventory scales will be developed so that they are balanced.

Messick and Jackson (1961a), by their use of degree of imbalance of "yesses" and "noes" as a proper index of acquiescence of course, imply that a balanced scale provides a proper control on this response style. In another, conjointly appearing paper, however, although largely agreeing with the effectiveness of the control on acquiescence achieved by a balanced scoring key, these authors open the door to quite another logic for operationalizing the concept of acquiescence. Jackson and Messick (1961) note the possibility that the "true" and "false" components of a scale, although balanced with respect to number of items, may yet "pull" differential amounts of variance. They suggest it is equalization of "true" and "false" variance in a scale that should be sought if the effect of acquiescence is to be considered eliminated because, in principle, a scale balanced with respect to the number of "trues" and "falses" it contains could be deriving all of its variance from only the "true" or only the "false" items.

However, this door to a new and presumably ultimate way of controlling acquiescence, although ajar, permits no reliable passage as was noted almost immediately: the "nuance (of equating the amounts of variance contributed by true-keyed and false-keyed items to a scale) could be achieved only with considerable labor, if at all" (Messick, 1962, p. 42). Yet, despite its unachievability and despite the significant control acknowledged as provided by balancing "yesses" and "noes", Messick has been reluctant to abandon this advocacy of hypothetical variance balancing: "A simple balancing of the number of true and false items . . . appears to provide important, but not always sufficient, insurance against the spurious influence of acquiescence response set upon total scores . . ." (Messick, 1962, p. 43). Astonishingly, Messick provides no operational rule by which the researcher may know when a balancing of the number of true- and false-keyed items excludes the adulterating effects of acquiescence and when it does not. It would appear that a "double-bind" has been created: the control we can achieve (of balancing the number of "yesses" and "noes") may always be threatened by a denial of sufficiency and by a demand for a control that cannot be achieved (the equation of variance contributions by the true- and false-keyed portions of a scale). This state of controlled ambiguity is, of course, insupportable. *Ad hoc* invocations cannot take the place of *a priori* criteria; a concept which cannot be stabilized by a set of operations can hardly prove useful.

In the primary analyses of MMPI scales to be reported in subsequent chapters, we have used scales balanced with respect to the number of "true" and "false" items. In one supplementary analysis, out of curiosity rather than conviction, the previously untried approach of balancing variance contributions was explored and found wanting. In choosing to ignore the significance of such differences as may arise between the "true" and "false" variance components of MMPI scales in favor of balancing item-keying, we have chosen for what we consider a superior logic, one that is established, incisive, and empirically testable. Much of what follows depends on balancing the number of "trues" and "falses" in MMPI scales as an adequate control for acquiescence; and the reader must at this juncture, or perhaps a bit later after reviewing some results derived within the variance-equalization approach, formulate his own judgment of the sufficiency of the control that has been employed.

With the approach of balancing responses thus argued for as both parsimonious and capable, how may we use it to unconfound *existing*, response-unbalanced scales? The way we have chosen to revise current MMPI scales so that acquiescence no longer may be said to contribute to the total score is to balance these scales as well, after the fact of their development. By dropping out, at random, enough items from the subset of "true" or "false" items predominating in a scale, a balanced scale may be derived. For example, the *Pt* scale of the MMPI contains 48 items, 39 of which are keyed in the "true" direction. Using a table of random numbers, 30 of the 39 "true"-keyed *Pt* items may be deleted leaving a shorter, 18 item *Pt* scale now balanced with 9 items keyed "true" and 9 items keyed "false."

It is important that the psychometric properties of MMPI scales balanced in this fashion be understood. Such scales will be shorter and therefore tend to be less reliable. The characteristics of these shorter scales depend on the conceptual model presumed to underlie the MMPI.

Some psychologists (Green, 1954; Jackson & Messick, 1961) project a "single common factor" view of MMPI scales. For them, the implicit mathematical model underlying an inventory scale presumes an *equivalence* or *interchangeability* of items, each item, in principle, contributing a small and equal amount of common variance toward the total score. Accordingly, by deleting items from a scale at random, what is measured by the scale does not change. Rather, the underlying psychological characteristic is measured less well. By this model, *the balanced scale measures precisely the same psychological content dimension measure by the longer, unbalanced scale but now—by virtue of the balancing—with acquiescence-response set eliminated.* How much less satisfactorily the balanced scale measures the original content dimension is an empirical question, to be answered by ascertaining the reliability of the shortened, balanced scale. As will be seen, most MMPI scales can be balanced and the reliabilities of the acquiescence-free MMPI scales remain acceptable.

A more complex view of the nature of MMPI scales is taken by psychologists steeped in knowledge of the origins and usage of the inventory. Thus, Harris (1962) has noted that in certain MMPI scales, there will be some shift or drift in psychological content as the scale is shortened and balanced. Different content areas within a particular MMPI scale have different frequencies of "true" and "false" answers because of accidents of phraseology in the MMPI-item pool, the avoidance of double negative, and intricate matters of language and psychopathology. Accordingly, deletion even at random from the preponderant set of items may be at the expense of a certain kind of content in a scale. However, and this is the crucial consideration, the shortened scale nevertheless eliminates the intrusion of a *content-independent* acquiescence-response set.[14]

With the recognition that current MMPI scales can be revised to eliminate their potential for reflecting an acquiescence compo-

---

[14] The notion of a content-*dependent* acquiescence-response set, recently proposed, would appear to trivialize the concept of acquiescence, depriving it of all parsimony and power.

nent, it, of course, becomes pertinent to analyze these revised scales to see whether the internal structure and external correlates of the balanced MMPI scales change radically. According to the acquiescence interpretation of the MMPI, the factor structure of the MMPI should change in fundamental respects if the acquiescence component is removed. To the extent that the acquiescence- or "yea-saying"-response style has personological significance, the behavioral syndrome previously identified (although confounded) with acquiescence should not relate to an acquiescence-free MMPI measure. On the other hand, if the claims for an acquiescence interpretation have capitalized, inadvertently, upon existing but by no means required imbalances in previous MMPI scales, then factor analysis of the set of balanced MMPI scales will reveal the same structure found when the scales are analyzed in their more conventional forms. The contrary hypotheses having been stated, let us turn to some data.

4

THE FACTOR STRUCTURE
UNDERLYING MMPI SCALES,
WITH ACQUIESCENCE
REMOVED AS A
CONTRIBUTING COMPONENT

A first decision involved fixing upon the set of MMPI scales to be analyzed in unbalanced and balanced forms. The eight usual "clinical" scales of the MMPI were included, together with the F and Si scales. The L scale which has 15 items, all keyed "false," and the K scale, whose 30 items include only one keyed "true", were both excluded. Obviously, neither of these scales can be balanced for they would be shortened to nothingness. Additional scales employed were: the Social Desirability (SD) scale (Edwards, 1957); the Ego-Strength (Es) scale (Barron, 1953); the Intellectual Efficiency (Ie) scale (Gough, 1957); the Leadership (Lp) scale (Oettel, 1953); the Social Participation (Sp) scale (Gough, 1952); the Social Status (St) scale (Gough, 1948); the Dominance (Do) scale (Gough, McClosky, & Meehl, 1951); the Social Introversion (Si) scale (Drake, 1946); and the Neurotic Under-Control (NUC) scale (Block, unpublished work presented in Dahlstrom & Welsh, 1960). Neither Welsh's A scale nor his R scale could be used in these analyses because, as earlier noted, they are not amenable to balancing. Instead, two scales developed some time ago by this writer to measure the first two factor dimensions of the MMPI in nonpathological populations

41

were substituted. These scales, labeled Psychoneurosis (*Pn*) and Ego-Control, Form 4 (*EC-4*), do permit balancing.[15] Their functional equivalence with the *A* and *R* scales is attested by correlations at about the limits set by the unreliabilities of the scales involved and so the interchange is warranted. Thus, a total of 21 scales was selected as representative of extant MMPI measures with respect to number, content, and kind of origin.

A balanced version of each of these 21 scales was derived in the manner just described. The number of items in each MMPI scale and its balanced version may be read from Table 6.

For each of five different samples, the following sequence of data analysis was applied:

1. The MMPI protocols were scored on the 21 unbalanced MMPI scales and on the 21 corresponding balanced versions of these scales.

2. The reliabilities (Kuder-Richardson Formula 20) of all scales were determined.

3. The correlation between each scale and its balanced version was calculated.

4. The 21 unbalanced MMPI scales and, *separately,* the 21 balanced MMPI scales were factor-analyzed by the principal-components method.

5. The comparability of the unrotated factor structures derived from analysis of the unbalanced and the balanced MMPI scales was assessed. Only the first two factors from each analysis were contrasted because, as noted earlier, the first two dimensions within the MMPI extract the great proportion of the communal variance. The factors were compared prior to rotation to eliminate all possibility of preferential positioning of the factor axes. It so happens that in four of the five samples studied, the unrotated factor dimensions are directly and even compellingly interpretable, as will be seen. But the reader should recall that any rigid translation of the factor axes will maintain invariant the relations among the variables being studied and, therefore, any conclusion derived from comparing unrotated factor structures will apply as well to these factor structures when they are comparably rotated. Although

[15] The items defining *Pn* and *NUC* are listed in Dahlstrom and Welsh (1960). The *Ec–4* scale is a slightly revised version of the scale identified (incorrectly) as *Eo* in that volume and is defined by the following item numbers: Keyed "true"—96, 111, 115, 133, 171, 183, 239, 289, 304, 329, 408, 493, and 503. Keyed "false"—59, 99, 118, 126, 149, 165, 181, 204, 208, 231, 254, 383, 400, 406, 441, 450, 451, 481, 491, and 529.

the equivalence of factors may often be judged sufficiently well simply by inspection, to objectify this comparison in the present study rank-order correlations were computed between the corresponding elements of the contrasted factors. In addition, the Wrigley-Neuhaus (1955) *coefficient of factorial similarity*—an index analogous to the product-moment correlation developed to express the congruence between the factors in the two studies—was calculated for each pair of corresponding factors.

The five samples studied may be briefly characterized:

1. 100 Air Force captains, with a mean age of 34.6.
2. 95 men, with a mean age of 38.9, who had participated in a study conducted at the Children's Hospital of the East Bay of familial factors in childhood diseases.
3. 46 men, with a modal age of 37, who had participated in the longitudinal study being carried out at the Institute of Human Development, Berkeley, California.
4. 110 women, with a mean age of 35.2, who had participated in the above mentioned study of familial factors in childhood diseases.
5. 49 women, with a modal age of 37, who had participated in the IHD longitudinal study.

Five different samples were employed so that the consistency of the results obtained could be evaluated. These particular samples were selected because of certain additional data available for them.

In Table 6 are presented the reliabilities of the MMPI scales being evaluated, for each of the five samples. The table displays the trends to be expected solely from psychometric considerations—the balanced scales tend to be somewhat less reliable than the original, unbalanced scales, the extent of drop in reliability being an approximate function of the extent of shortening of the scale. The reliabilities of the acquiescence-removed balanced scale, however, although lower because of scale shortening, are not fundamentally changed.

Table 6 also contains the correlations, for each sample, between each unbalanced scale and its corresponding balanced version. These are part-whole correlations since all the items in the balanced scale are contained also in the unbalanced scale. But this is as it should be, given the logic of balancing. The resulting

TABLE 6

Descriptive Characteristics of the 21 MMPI Scales Studied

Scale	Number of items in unbalanced scale	Reliabilities of unbalanced scales	Number of items in balanced scale	Reliabilities of balanced scales	Correlations of unbalanced and balanced scales
F	64	.45, .58, .50, .66, .64	40	.40, .53, .49, .40, .67	.83, .91, .87, .93, .96
Hs	33	.69, .66, .75, .82, .85	22	.64, .55, .68, .78, .82	.93, .89, .94, .95, .97
D	60	.42, .42, .50, .62, .74	40	.24, .31, .53, .62, .74	.84, .82, .88, .91, .93
Hy	60	.32, .60, .71, .41, .70	26	.08, .42, .52, .37, .64	.68, .73, .86, .77, .88
Pd	50	.36, .48, .50, .51, .61	48	.38, .47, .49, .50, .62	.99, .99, .99, .99, .99
Mf	60	.37, .62, .61, .48, .44	56	.40, .58, .62, .50, .53	.98, .99, .98, .96, .95
Pa	40	.20, .26, .25, .26, .35	30	.08, .30, .22, .23, .09	.90, .91, .91, .90, .90
Pt	48	.81, .80, .83, .88, .91	18	.61, .54, .54, .75, .75	.90, .85, .86, .93, .91
Sc	78	.73, .78, .69, .87, .90	38	.37, .58, .24, .68, .75	.78, .83, .60, .91, .95
Ma	46	.59, .55, .51, .49, .57	22	.21, .37, .20, −.05, .37	.78, .76, .80, .69, .82
Pn	33	.86, .69, .74, .80, .80	20	.80, .57, .65, .68, .70	.94, .89, .89, .92, .91
SD	39	.70, .76, .79, .83, .86	18	.58, .61, .64, .69, .74	.86, .89, .90, .92, .94
Es	68	.53, .61, .54, .68, .78	50	.38, .36, .43, .50, .69	.89, .87, .89, .93, .96
Ie	39	.62, .67, .58, .68, .76	30	.61, .61, .50, .64, .73	.96, .96, .97, .97, .97
Lp	50	.72, .72, .83, .82, .84	28	.57, .51, .61, .67, .70	.84, .86, .92, .91, .93
Sp	25	.56, .66, .56, .69, .65	16	.45, .58, .50, .59, .60	.91, .90, .93, .93, .93
St	34	.48, .59, .50, .65, .56	30	.48, .55, .48, .60, .48	.99, .97, .98, .98, .97
Do	28	.33, .62, .37, .59, .58	14	.19, .30, .07, .20, .28	.79, .82, .81, .80, .82
Si	70	.76, .77, .87, .85, .88	68	.76, .77, .87, .85, .88	1.00, 1.00, 1.00, 1.00, 1.00
EC-4	33	.70, .64, .62, .46, .58	26	.55, .49, .44, .16, .50	.96, .95, .94, .91, .95
NUC	33	.82, .76, .56, .76, .69	17*	.69, .49, .33, .56, .43	.92, .89, .80, .87, .88

* It was discovered, after the present analyses were well under way, that the balanced version of the *NUC* scale was in slight error, containing one too many statements keyed "true." This mistake does not affect the sense or substance of the present findings in any significant way.

TABLE 7

The First Two Unrotated Dimensions Derived from Separate Factor Analyses of Unbalanced and Balanced MMPI Scales, Sample A

Scale	Unbalanced MMPI		Balanced MMPI	
	Factor 1	Factor 2	Factor 1	Factor 2
F	−.59	−.20	−.37	−.26
Hs	−.79	.13	−.77	.04
D	−.24	.44	−.51	.14
Hy	.19	.26	.00	.16
Pd	−.35	−.35	−.32	−.39
Mf	−.31	−.31	−.28	−.44
Pa	−.10	−.02	.10	.11
Pt	−.89	−.10	−.82	−.21
Sc	−.85	−.23	−.68	−.10
Ma	−.46	−.65	−.04	−.71
Pn	−.90	.01	−.83	−.12
SD	.89	−.06	.82	−.07
Es	.59	−.19	.43	−.25
Ie	.61	−.18	.57	−.08
Lp	.80	−.22	.77	−.04
Sp	.42	−.58	.48	−.51
St	.17	−.63	.19	−.67
Do	.48	−.22	.19	−.30
Si	−.56	.56	−.67	.39
EC-4	.21	.81	.04	.80
NUC	−.72	−.43	−.56	−.49

high correlations reflect no artifact but rather are proper indicators of the extent to which the balanced scales have the same psychological meaning—but with acquiescence removed—as the scales from which they derive. These high correlations between corresponding unbalanced and balanced scales also foretell (indeed, entail) the results obtained through factor analysis.

We note that the results of Table 6 do not appear to be due to any special characteristics of the set of balanced MMPI scoring templates used. It will be recalled that a random basis was employed to delete the necessary number of items scored in the predominant direction. Although methodologically our design would have been improved somewhat if for each subject in each sample a unique set of randomly balanced templates had been used, this formidable nicety was disregarded after preliminary checks showed impressive consistency of scores over different versions of equivalently-constituted balanced scales.

TABLE 8

The First Two Unrotated Dimensions Derived from Separate Factor Analyses of Unbalanced and Balanced MMPI Scales, Sample B

| | Unbalanced MMPI | | Balanced MMPI | |
Scale	*Factor 1*	*Factor 2*	*Factor 1*	*Factor 2*
F	−.62	−.24	−.48	−.22
Hs	−.57	−.30	−.66	−.17
D	−.42	−.19	−.67	−.26
Hy	.27	−.44	.06	−.38
Pd	−.45	−.51	−.49	−.46
Mf	−.14	−.61	−.19	−.62
Pa	−.12	−.39	.03	−.27
Pt	−.88	−.27	−.72	−.36
Sc	−.81	−.35	−.70	−.22
Ma	−.35	−.52	−.04	−.61
Pn	−.82	−.04	−.70	−.17
SD	.89	.02	.82	−.02
Es	.62	−.09	.43	−.10
Ie	.76	−.29	.73	−.19
Lp	.75	−.26	.70	−.17
Sp	.57	−.41	.57	−.51
St	.50	−.67	.43	−.71
Do	.65	−.45	.36	−.41
Si	−.64	.46	−.68	.47
EC-4	.10	.69	.06	.74
NUC	−.70	−.20	−.59	−.12

In Tables, 7, 8, 9, 10, and 11 are presented, for each of the five samples studied, the first two factors derived from the unbalanced MMPI scales and the first two factors derived from the balanced versions of these scales. By inspection, *it is indisputably clear that the factor structure of the MMPI does not change when the possibility of interference from an acquiescence-response set is removed.* Table 12 summarizes the rank-order correlations and Wrigley-Neubaus coefficients between corresponding factors.

TABLE 9

The First Two Unrotated Dimensions Derived from Separate Factor Analyses of Unbalanced and Balanced MMPI Scales, Sample C

	Unbalanced MMPI		Balanced MMPI	
Scale	*Factor 1*	*Factor 2*	*Factor 1*	*Factor 2*
F	−.57	−.38	−.52	−.05
Hs	−.46	−.49	−.42	−.53
D	−.61	.14	−.69	−.23
Hy	−.10	−.52	−.06	−.63
Pd	−.37	−.67	−.34	−.56
Mf	−.30	−.36	−.26	−.32
Pa	.00	−.39	.27	−.37
Pt	−.89	−.19	−.77	−.41
Sc	−.76	−.38	−.50	−.13
Ma	−.25	−.70	−.04	−.55
Pn	−.79	−.13	−.68	−.31
SD	.87	.01	.71	.07
Es	.51	.10	.40	.04
Ie	.70	−.06	.75	.05
Lp	.81	−.36	.76	−.24
Sp	.55	−.49	.66	−.40
St	.62	−.57	.60	−.54
Do	.61	−.20	.33	−.21
Si	−.72	.61	−.76	.54
EC-4	−.35	.68	−.39	.48
NUC	−.65	−.28	−.55	−.17

These correlations are strikingly high. The first factor is identical in both analyses; the second factor blurs very slightly when the shorter, balanced scales are employed—perhaps because less variance is involved in its definition—but still remains in indisputable focus.

In Samples A, B, D, and E, the factor structures are impressively parallel. In the fifth instance, involving Sample C, the internal structure of the MMPI appears to be somewhat different

TABLE 10

The First Two Unrotated Dimensions Derived from Separate Factor Analyses of Unbalanced and Balanced MMPI Scales, Sample D

Scale	Unbalanced MMPI		Balanced MMPI	
	Factor 1	Factor 2	Factor 1	Factor 2
F	−.62	−.20	−.57	−.07
Hs	−.75	−.25	−.76	−.28
D	−.71	−.06	−.76	−.26
Hy	−.13	−.48	−.30	−.45
Pd	−.51	−.37	−.53	−.35
Mf	.09	−.44	.17	−.51
Pa	−.28	−.35	−.09	−.31
Pt	−.93	−.12	−.88	−.18
Sc	−.85	−.29	−.77	−.24
Ma	−.38	−.52	−.02	−.49
Pn	−.79	−.04	−.72	−.13
SD	.92	.04	.83	.03
Es	.82	.16	.72	.18
Ie	.85	−.21	.82	−.17
Lp	.82	−.21	.79	−.17
Sp	.68	−.45	.72	−.43
St	.58	−.53	.55	−.53
Do	.71	−.31	.38	−.34
Si	−.77	.42	−.78	.34
EC-4	.04	.56	−.11	.53
NUC	−.78	−.07	−.68	−.04

than that observed in the other samples. In this sample alone, a sizable third factor exists and a rotation of the axes improves the factorial simplicity of the measures. When the three factors found within Sample C are rotated by the Varimax method (Kaiser, 1958), the first two factors in the resulting factor structure prove to show appreciable concordance with the first two unrotated factors found in the other four samples. Table 13 presents for the balanced scales analysis of Sample C, the factor structure existing

TABLE 11

The First Two Unrotated Dimensions Derived from Separate Factor Analyses of Unbalanced and Balanced MMPI Scales, Sample E

| | Unbalanced MMPI | | Balanced MMPI | |
Scale	Factor 1	Factor 2	Factor 1	Factor 2
F	−.67	−.24	−.63	−.20
Hs	−.83	−.28	−.84	−.26
D	−.84	.07	−.85	−.04
Hy	−.47	−.54	−.58	−.35
Pd	−.63	−.61	−.67	−.56
Mf	−.15	−.32	−.01	−.41
Pa	−.40	−.42	−.24	−.53
Pt	−.96	−.06	−.88	−.11
Sc	−.89	−.25	−.82	−.31
Ma	−.28	−.75	.03	−.79
Pn	−.85	−.11	−.81	−.19
SD	.92	−.15	.89	−.15
Es	.85	.01	.76	.02
Ie	.77	−.05	.77	−.08
Lp	.79	−.41	.75	−.33
Sp	.68	−.50	.65	−.51
St	.77	−.37	.74	−.35
Do	.74	−.38	.41	−.34
Si	−.77	.50	−.76	.49
EC-4	−.12	.65	−.10	.63
NUC	−.70	−.13	−.57	−.03

TABLE 12

The Comparability of Corresponding Factors for the Five Samples Studied

	Correlation of Unbalanced Factor 1 with Balanced Factor 1	*Correlation of Unbalanced Factor 2 with Balanced Factor 2*
Sample A	.96 (.95)	.92 (.95)
Sample B	.96 (.97)	.87 (.98)
Sample C	.97 (.98)	.82 (.93)
Sample D	.96 (.98)	.95 (.98)
Sample E	.97 (.99)	.95 (.98)

NOTE: The figures in parentheses are *coefficients of factorial similarity.*

after this rotation. Comparison of the first two factors in the rotated structure with the corresponding unrotated factors of Sample C (Table 9) reveals an appreciable gain in the factorial clarity of the second dimension, accompanied by a further, slight improvement in the already clear understanding of the first factor. It should be noted that for subsequent interpretations and analyses stemming from the factor-analytic results for Sample C, the first two factors *after* rotation are being employed because of their greater congruence with the unrotated factors found in the other four samples. The third factor found within Sample C, although of potential significance, was not further considered in this study.

The independent psychological significance of these repetitively found MMPI dimensions is explored in Chapter 8 of this monograph, but at this juncture a brief assay of the factors found in the acquiescence-removed analyses is useful. For those knowledgeable of earlier factor analyses of the MMPI, no great surprises will be occasioned by our results. The first factor underlying the balanced scales, to which we give for the present the noncommittal name of Alpha, is defined at its negative end by a cluster of scales purporting to reflect a neurotic and maladaptive

TABLE 13

The First Three Factors Derived from Factor Analysis of Balanced MMPI Scales, after Varimax Rotation, Sample C

Scale	Factor 1	Factor 2	Factor 3
F	−.55	.07	−.30
Hs	−.52	.18	.46
D	−.58	.45	.15
Hy	−.21	.09	.77
Pd	−.61	−.13	.24
Mf	−.45	−.12	.03
Pa	.14	−.09	.56
Pt	−.83	.25	.10
Sc	−.47	.21	−.05
Ma	−.35	−.25	.35
Pn	−.66	.33	.14
SD	.66	−.26	.24
Es	.13	−.58	−.30
Ie	.50	−.62	−.07
Lp	.55	−.39	.50
Sp	.25	−.64	.36
St	.11	−.70	.42
Do	.00	−.55	−.04
Si	−.30	.68	−.56
EC-4	.13	.75	−.11
NUC	−.69	−.07	−.33

character structure (*e.g., Pt, Sc, Pn*) and at the other end by scales, led by Edwards' SD measure, which relate to a more self-satisfied and culturally valued adjustive mode (*e.g., Lp, Sp, St, Ie*). Alpha is very well—perhaps too well—measured by MMPI scales and much economy would be introduced by settling on but one or two of these scales to represent this dimension.

For Edwards, Alpha is the Social Desirability dimension; for Welsh, the preferred label for this dimension (reversed) is Anxiety; for earlier MMPI workers, this component—usually indexed by twin peaks on the *Pt* and *Sc* scales—has been interpreted as relating to an agitated despair imbedded within a neurotic character structure.

The second factor emerging from the analyses of the balanced scales, temporarily labeled Beta, is the dimension that formerly —when confounding existed—was often construed as strongly reflecting acquiescence-response set (Jackson & Messick, 1961; Jackson & Messick, 1962; Edwards, Diers, & Walker, 1962). Now, with the exclusion of interference from an acquiescence component and from knowledge of the external criteria used to establish its defining measures, Beta can be identified as relating to the way individuals characteristically monitor their impulses. At one end of the dimension is a scale specifically measuring over-control (*EC-4*), and at the other end a few scales related to impulse expression and social expansiveness (*e.g., Ma, Sp, St, Pd*). Beta is not so redundantly measured within the MMPI as is the first factor largely because, as will be seen, the MMPI-item pool contains comparatively few items pertinent to this dimension. Welsh's second factor, from which he derived his *R* (repression) scale, clearly is akin to this dimension; the writer earlier has preferred to conceptualize the Beta continuum as *ego-control*. A larger effort to understand and interpret this MMPI factor is best deferred until after an examination of its behavioral correlates.

To summarize matters at this point in our analytical progression, we may clearly affirm the inconsequentiality of acquiescence-response set insofar as the factorial structure of the MMPI is concerned. Comparison of the factor structure of the MMPI when acquiescence conceivably could be operating with the factor structure existing when acquiescence is denied effect reveals an astonishing parallelism. If the present five samples may be taken as a basis for generalization, it follows that the impact of acquiescence is so minute as to often not warrant the complications attendant upon excluding its effect. Previous work employing unbalanced MMPI scales appears not to have been vitiated by failure to consider the possible contribution of acquiescence; subsequent researchers employing the MMPI will have to decide for themselves whether the gains of using balanced scales outweigh the possible costs of thereby excluding from usage numerous valid items which cannot be balanced within the existing item pool.

As an addendum to this chapter, we report on an empirical exploration of the Messick and Jackson suggestion that the influence of acquiescence is eliminated only if the variances of the "true" and "false" subscales comprising a full scale are equalized.[16] Only those readers detailedly involved in these matters may wish to complete the next few pages.

The twenty-one full-length MMPI scales already described and used in preceding analyses were partitioned into their "true" and "false" subscales. The variances of each pair of subscales were calculated on Sample A and then, by trial-and-error deletions of items from the subscale with the larger variance, this subscale was shortened so that its variance closely matched that of its conversely-keyed partner. The variance adjusting process was tedious and involved repeated scorings of various versions of the subscales on Sample A. The pairs of variances finally achieved were well equated, as attested by an average variance ratio of 1.031, with a range from 1.004 to 1.066. Of course, in achieving equalization of subscale variances, the desideratum of balancing item-keying of necessity had to be abandoned. The mean ratio of response imbalance, after variance balancing in Sample A, was 1.39, with a range from 1.00 to 2.08.

After variance equalization, the resulting "true" and "false" subscales were combined again to form twenty-one modified MMPI scales in each of which, according to the shifted Messick and Jackson position, the influence of an acquiescent response set should be completely excluded. These scales were then factor-analyzed as before, with the first two factors again proving dominant. These two factors were related to the factors issuing from the factor analysis of these scales in their original form and again, a most impressive correspondence is to be seen. The rank-order correlations between the first factors from the two analyses was .91 and for the second factors was .82; the Wrigley-Neuhaus

[16] The idea of comparing the factor structure of variance-equalized scales with the factor structure of these scales in their original form is due to Dr. Lewis Goldberg. It was more convenient for me than for him to carry out the required analyses and, at his urging, I have included them here. I am grateful to him for the suggestion.

coefficients of factorial similarity beween the corresponding factors were .90 and .89, respectively. Clearly, after variance-equalization as well as after response-balancing, the factor structure of the MMPI remains unchanged. By either approach to unconfounding, an interpretation in terms of acquiescent response set is voided.

Having shown that variance-equalization, when applied, does not change the implication of results drawn from response-balanced analyses, we may now go on to show why the variance-equalization approach envisioned by Messick is, in a fundamental sense, unsatisfactory. Consider what happens when laboriously matched "true" and "false" subscales are applied to samples other than the one on which the matching is based. Thus, when Samples B through E are scored on the subscales equalized with respect to Sample A, the equalization at once disappears. The mean variance ratios for these latter four samples are, respectively 1.404, 1.348, 1.575, and 2.191. Individual variance ratios are as high as 6.698!

Invariant variance-equalization is, as was anticipated, unachievable. Of course, variance-balancing within each sample to tailor subscales to conform to the characteristics of each particular aggregation of subjects can be done but the results of these endeavors, foretold by the results achieved with Sample A and by part-whole considerations, would again have no generality. If we are concerned with acquiescence as a quality or characteristic differentially held by individuals which, often as a nuisance, intrudes upon our measurement of other behavioral dimensions, then we require a method of controlling its manifestations so these other facets of behavior may be clearly seen. This method of controlling acquiescence must prevent the responding subject from earning a scale score because of certain acquiescent tendencies and so *this control must exist independent of and logically prior to the response of the subject to the inventory items.* Response-balancing of scales fulfills this requirement and is a general procedure.

However, variance-balancing provides an *intra-group* rather than an *intra-individual* adjustment. It is achieved after the fact of response and depends upon responses other than those of the particular subject in order to determine the required "correction." The "acquiescence-free" scores an individual is awarded through variance-balancing are an undefined and chancy function of the subject sample within which he happens to be evaluated. His scores will be interpreted differently if the sample—not the subject—changes. Thus, a subject from a sample in which variance-balancing has been accomplished will appear as an acquiescer when scored vis-à-vis a second sample and as a non-acquiescer when scored amidst the variance proclivities of still another sample although his own item responses remain unchanged. The conceptual utility or integrating capacity of acquiescence, defined so transiently, can hardly be great.

5

THE ACQUIESCENCE INTERPRETATION AS AN ACCIDENTAL CONSEQUENCE OF SOME CHARACTERISTICS OF THE MMPI-ITEM POOL

Having shown that when acquiescence is prevented from intruding, the internal structure of the MMPI remains the same, we are left with the insistent question: Why did the MMPI scales, when they were initially constructed, prove to be so unbalanced and in ways admitting of an interpretation in terms of acquiescence-response set?

To help unravel this woolly matter, a number of additional analyses were executed. Within each of the five samples, a group of Alpha Highs and a group of Alpha Lows were designated based upon the factor scores which were available for each individual. Factor scores were computed using the Holzinger-Harman short-form method which weights the factor-score contribution of each scale according to its factor loading. Then, for each sample, the MMPI-response protocols of the Alpha Highs were contrasted with the MMPI-response protocols of the Alpha Lows in order to identify, by means of a differential frequency of response, the items which distinguish the two groups. Additionally, the Alpha Highs from the five samples were combined and their MMPI answers compared with those of the combined groups of Alpha Lows.

Now, the Alpha dimension was derived from analysis of *balanced* MMPI scales and therefore, high and low scorers on this dimension have earned their placement uninfluenced by an acquiescence-response set. Accordingly, the simple hypothesis might follow that when only the items differentiating Alpha Highs from Alpha Lows are examined, there should be about as many items responded to more affirmatively (*i.e.*, with greater frequency) by the Alpha Highs as there are items responded to more affirmatively by Alpha Lows. In other words, a scale to measure the Alpha dimension based upon contrasting, via item-analytic procedures, groups of Alpha Highs and of Alpha Lows would be expected, by the null hypothesis, to have as many responses keyed "true" as are keyed "false."

For the item-analyses, Fisher's exact method for testing the significance of 2×2 contingency tables was used, the criterion for considering an item as discriminating being set at the .05 level. It should be noted that, as reported elsewhere (Block, 1960), only about 1.7 or 2% of the MMPI items should reach the .05 level of

TABLE 14

Summary Results of Item Analysis of Alpha Highs versus Alpha Lows

Sample	Number of Alpha Highs	Number of Alpha Lows	Number signif- icant at .05 level	Percent signif- icant at .05 level	Number answered more affirm- atively by Alpha Highs	Number answered more affirm- atively by Alpha Lows
A	20	20	130	22.97	32	98
B	19	20	112	19.79	25	87
C	17	17	32	5.65	5	27
D	20	20	208	36.75	58	150
E	18	13	76	13.43	25	51
Combined Samples	95	97	355	62.72	100	255

NOTE: The slight inconsistency between the *N*'s reported for the combined samples (95 and 97) as compared to the *N*'s calculated by summing over the individual samples (94 and 90) derive from a slight change, for the last item analysis, in the cutting points used to determine Alpha Highs and Alpha Lows.

significance by chance when a nonpsychiatric sample is being studied. Table 14 presents the summary results of these analyses.

Equivalent item-analyses of the Beta dimension were carried out after groups of Beta Highs and Beta Lows were formed. The five groups of Beta Highs, combined, were also contrasted with the combined groups of Beta Lows. The summary results of these analyses may be read from Table 15. Again, the expectation would be that, because acquiescence had no influence upon the

TABLE 15

Summary Results of Item Analyses of Beta Highs versus Beta Lows

Sample	Number of Beta Highs	Number of Beta Lows	Number significant at .05 level	Percent significant at .05 level	Number answered more affirmatively by Beta Highs	Number answered more affirmatively by Beta Lows
A	20	20	50	8.83	6	44
B	20	21	49	8.66	24	25
C	17	17	53	9.36	21	32
D	20	20	46	8.13	19	27
E	16	17	27	4.77	18	9
Combined Samples	97	98	138	24.38	45	93

NOTE: The slight inconsistency between the *N*'s reported for the combined samples (97 and 98) as compared to the *N*'s calculated by summing over the individual samples (93 and 95) derive from a slight change, for the last item analysis, in the cutting points used to determine Beta Highs and Beta Lows.

Beta dimension, Beta Highs should be as "yea-saying" as Beta Lows.

Before considering the implications of each table separately, it is illuminating to compare the analyses of Alpha with the analyses of Beta. It may be seen that the Alpha dimension is profusely represented within the MMPI-item pool and that the Beta dimension, although not "pulling" nearly so many items, also constellates a nonchance set of items.

If the informal criterion of the number of items reaching the

.05 level of significance is taken to indicate the extent of representation of a dimension within the item pool, then the Alpha dimension carries about three times the influence of the Beta dimension within the MMPI. Indeed, the number of items strongly associated with the Alpha dimension is astonishing—about 63% significant at the .05 level when sizable groups are compared. This redundancy far exceeds the requirements of good measurement and, coupled with the item-overlap problem previously mentioned, clarifies why the first factor underlying MMPI scales is so dominant, leaving little MMPI-scale variance remaining.

It should be noted that, although earlier evidence and the results we shall report in Chapter 8 testify to the behavioral significance of the Alpha dimension within the MMPI, it does not follow that this redundantly-indexed MMPI component is *behaviorally* more important than other MMPI factors which are less distinctly specified within the MMPI-item pool. Indeed, our results will show that in nonpsychiatric samples, the Beta dimension relates to behavior as pervasively as does the Alpha dimension.

Yet, in fairness to the MMPI and the rationale underlying its construction, it must be recognized that in psychiatric samples (for which the inventory was developed), the apparent redundancy of the measurement of the Alpha dimension may be warranted if subfactors or groupings of symptoms related to psychiatric entities are found to exist within the sprawling domain of Alpha. These subfactors are not so readily discernible when nonpsychiatric samples are being studied or when factor analysis is applied at the scale rather than at the item or subscale level.

Looking next at the results polarized by the Alpha dimension, it may be seen that the item-analyses reveal an intrinsic imbalance in the constitution of the MMPI-item pool—in each of the five samples, many more items are answered affirmatively by Alpha Lows than are affirmed by Alpha Highs. The trend is consistent, strong, and highly significant statistically. If an MMPI scale to measure the Alpha dimension were comprised of the items discriminating Alpha Highs from Alpha Lows—a conventional and reasonable procedure for constructing personality scales—the resulting measure (if scored for Alpha Highs) would have about one-fourth of its items keyed for "true" and three-fourths of its items keyed for "false." Thus, although our procedures averted the influence of any effect of an agreement-response set, because the MMPI-item pool happens to contain relatively few items affirmable by Alpha Highs and many items declarable by Alpha Lows, Alpha Highs will appear to be "nay-sayers" and Alpha Lows "yea-sayers." A seeming manifestation of acquiescence has reappeared which, under less understood circumstances, might have been taken as evidence for the operation of this response set.

In the light of these results, it is retrospectively clear why the MMPI scales which relate to the Alpha dimension have, to a greater or lesser degree, an imbalance in their keying. The Sc scale, loading strongly on the Alpha dimension and aimed to measure the negative end of that continuum, contains 59 items keyed "true" and only 19 items keyed "false"; the SD scale, a superb measure of the positive end of the Alpha, contains 9 items keyed "true" but 30 items keyed "false." Both of these scales (and many others) have been claimed for acquiescence in the past and it is now clear how this misconstruction came about. By manipulating—deliberately or not—the loading of an MMPI scale on the Alpha dimension, the extent of item imbalance in that scale can also be expected to vary systematically.

The interpretation of the first factor of the MMPI in terms of acquiescence as once proposed by Messick and Jackson (1961a) may be seen now to have been seemingly feasible because of these intrinsic properties of the MMPI-item pool. The origins of this preponderance of items phrased in the one direction rather than in the other with respect to the Alpha dimension cannot be fully identified—it lies in part in some deliberate decisions made when constituting the item pool, in part in the extraordinary difficulty of phrasing certain statements in reverse form and, doubtless, in part in the way the MMPI just happened to evolve.

Although the result was foregone, the social desirability scale values of the items significantly related to the Alpha dimension were ascertained by making reference to the recent Messick and Jackson (1961b) social desirability scaling of the MMPI. In the main, the items affirmable by the Alpha Highs were highly desirable socially and the items "acquiesced" to by Alpha Lows were undesirable. Comparatively few items with intermediate social desirability values proved significant.

The analyses for the Beta dimension do not show so simple or potent a trend in the way the discriminating items are allocated to Beta Highs and Beta Lows, perhaps because the Beta dimension is not so weightily represented in the MMPI. There is a tendency for Beta Lows to be "yea-sayers" but the relationship is not so striking as for the Alpha dimension. The "yea-saying" ratios of Beta Lows are somewhat, but not greatly, accentuated if the Beta-related items which are highly desirable or highly undesirable socially are excluded from consideration. These latter items tend to be tinged heavily with Alpha. When only the items having SD scale values in the middle-two intervals of the eight-interval scaling continuum are considered, the number of affirmable items for Beta Highs and for Beta Lows becomes, for the five samples respectively, 1:23; 11:16; 7:14; 6:13; and 7:4. For combined samples, the ratio becomes 20:48.

It may well be that the characteristics of the MMPI-item pool, in conjunction with some other understandings, provides a basis for explaining the contentual core of "maladaptive under-control" which appears to underlie the Dy-3 scale of Jackson and Messick. In constituting the Dy-3 scale, they selected items falling within the midrange of the social desirability continuum. Comparatively few items related to the Alpha dimension will be selected by this criterion while the likelihood of the selection of Beta-relevant items is increased. With the power of the Alpha dimension lessened (but by no means eliminated), the relatively under-weighted Beta dimension is accentuated in importance and can take greater (but not complete) charge of the Dy-3 scale. Thus, when the correlations of Dy-3 with the *balanced* MMPI scales are calculated, it is found in all five samples that the Dy-3 scale falls within the Alpha Low-Beta Low quadrant.

As a consequence of the imbalance in keying of the Alpha-relevant and Beta-relevant items so that the low ends of *both* the Alpha and Beta dimensions are more densely represented by MMPI items than are the high ends, it follows that high scorers on a scale located in the Alpha Low-Beta Low quadrant (*e.g.*, the Dy-3 scale) will—unless further controls are instituted—naturally be responding with "yesses" much more often than with "noes." That is, a scale located in the Alpha Low-Beta Low quadrant "fuses" or cumulates the response imbalances of both dimensions and therefore would be composed of items keyed primarily, but not exclusively, for "trues." This predicted description fits the *Dy-3* scale well for it will be remembered that about one-third of the item intercorrelations in the *Dy-3* scale were negative, indicating "true" keying for these items was inappropriate. Finally, if a low position on the Alpha dimension is viewed for the present as signifying "neuroticism" and a low position on Beta is termed indicative of "under-control," then the contentual core of "maladaptive under-control" observed as the dominant factor in the *Dy-3* scale is explained. This complicated rationale will perhaps achieve its final support in Chapter 8, when the personological correlates of the Alpha and Beta dimensions are explored.

In summary, the analyses of Highs and Lows on the Alpha and Beta dimensions afford the following recognitions. There is probably an overweighting of the Alpha dimension within the MMPI and perhaps an underrepresentation of the Beta dimension. The difficulty in establishing sizable and reliable factors beyond the first two components when analyzing MMPI scales may be ascribed, in large part, to a redundancy of the basic item pool. This redundancy may redeem itself when the MMPI is applied solely to psychiatric populations; when used in nonpsychiatric settings, however, the MMPI-item pool appears to be too narrow in its coverage or weighting of dimensions beyond Alpha. Because of the structural properties of the MMPI-item pool, Alpha Lows particularly but also Beta Lows will appear—unfairly—to be acquiescent. The items related to the Beta dimension tend to be of intermediate social desirability value while the items related to the Alpha dimension usually are at extremes of the social desirability scale continuum. The contentual core of the *Dy-3* scale can be viewed as a fortuitous function of the characteristics of the MMPI-item pool.

Having shown that acquiescence is not an important determinant of MMPI responses and how the credibility of the acquiescence interpretation happened to evolve as a function of the intrinsic characteristics of the MMPI-item pool, we may set this response style aside and focus now on social desirability.

6

SOME DIFFICULTIES WITH THE SOCIAL DESIRABILITY INTERPRETATION OF THE MMPI

In this chapter, we shall be concerned with Edwards' notion of social desirability (SD) insofar as it pertains to the MMPI. The concept of SD has been applied as well toward the explanation of other tests and procedures but generalization of the arguments against SD to be developed in this chapter—although believed to be feasible—would be digressive and will not be attempted within these confines. We also note that certain of the points to be made have been made before, in the literature and elsewhere —here we collect them and add some others.

What specifically does Edwards mean by social desirability? The term, SD, is used by Edwards in two interrelated ways. The first sense of the concept has reference simply to the SD scale values of inventory items as developed via a competent scaling method using an appropriate set of judges (*e.g.*, Heineman, 1952; Messick & Jackson, 1961b). The second and more ambitious usage of SD refers to "the tendency of subjects to attribute to themselves, in self-description, personality statements with socially desirable scale values and to reject those with socially undesirable scale values" (Edwards, 1957, p. vi). An alternative, and explicitly equivalent, definition of the social desirability response tendency (SDRT) is "faking good on personality inventories, *without special instructions to do so*" (Edwards, 1957, p. 57) (italics added).

It is important to recognize that Edwards does not mean by SDRT that *deliberate* lying is involved. Repeatedly, he has argued and shown (*e.g.*, Edwards, 1957; Edwards, Dier, & Walker, 1962) that intentional "faking good" is importantly different from SD. Other studies, as summarized by Wiggins (1962), bear him out. The implications of the concept, SDRT, as drawn by Edwards, should be understood as involving a genuine dissimulation but one which is not—at least usually—at the level of awareness of the responding individual. Edwards does not deny that an individual's SDRT can be enhanced by a deliberate set to do so, or be minimized—such changes are simply not a defining characteristic of SDRT for him. Edwards (1957, p. 58) even anticipated the comparative ineffectiveness of his *SD* scale in identifying deliberate efforts to "fake good" (Wiggins, 1959). This latter demonstration is in keeping with other, distinctively different and less encompassing conceptions of SD and does not gainsay Edwards' definition and orientation in terms of a *spontaneously* employed SDRT.

The possibility, and even the likelihood, of faking in the MMPI was recognized early (*e.g.*, Meehl & Hathaway, 1946; Cofer, Chance, & Judson, 1949) and, prior to Edwards, the approach to this problem was to qualify the interpretation of the MMPI as a function of the amount and kind of faking which had been identified. Edwards has been more audacious. Here is his position:

1. He has contended that the SD dimension, as defined by him, is the most important single dimension in terms of which to view responses to personality inventories and that subjects respond to inventories such as the MMPI primarily in ways determined by their personal SDRTs. It is worth noting here that although acquiescence was a response style independent of content, the SD-response set cannot be maintained without an orientation toward the content of the items being answered. The SD interpretation singles out one of many possible facets of meaning and asserts that this aspect of consistent response overrides the importance of

other content dimensions in determining inventory responses (Edwards, 1957).

2. The contribution of SD is viewed by Edwards as distorting because the SD-content dimension is postulated as characterologically irrelevant or superficial. Since SD is so dominant a determinant of MMPI response, Edwards has argued vigorously against interpretation of the MMPI as related to psychologically significant behaviors. Instead, he suggests that the social desirability variable is a parsimonious and quite sufficient operational explanation of the MMPI which escapes from the vague, psychodynamic interpretations previously advanced. Writing of efforts to continue with a psychological interpretation of the massive first factor of the MMPI, he (with Walker) says:

> We do not believe that these and various other reinterpretations of the social desirability variable serve to clarify matters in any degree, although the new labels may be more satisfying to the psychologist who is clinically and dynamically oriented. We have nothing against personality dynamics, but we do not believe they should be invoked when relatively simply psychometric considerations are adequate to account for the correlations that have been found between various personality scales and the SD. . . . So also can the first factor loadings of the MMPI scales be accounted for in terms of the zero-order correlations of the MMPI scales with the SD (Edwards & Walker, 1961b, p. 182).

3. Edwards (1959, p. 115) has presupposed that social desirability should be eliminated from or at least controlled in personality inventories like the MMPI if validity is to be enhanced. He is pessimistic, however, about finding much beyond error variance once the SD factor is extracted. On other occasions, he has been willing to interpret the second factor of the MMPI as an acquiescence component after emphasizing that the first—and primary—factor is best understood in terms of SD (Edwards & Walker, 1961b). In a tour de force, Edwards and Walker (1961c) have gone so far as to suggest the SD scale may be used as a short form of the MMPI because, from the SD scores of a sample of college students, they were able to predict with great accuracy the ordering of scores achieved by each of a number of subjects when their MMPI's were scored on a selected set of MMPI scales.

What is the evidence adduced in support of SD's centrality in understanding the MMPI? Two kinds of demonstrations have been employed and replicated with only minor variations. The first of these is the accumulation of many findings that an SD measure correlates highly and even perfectly with certain MMPI scales and can be used as a marker or reference variable in factor analyses of MMPI scales. The second basis for asserting the importance of SD is the observation that the *proportion* of subjects who acknowledge an inventory item as applicable in self-description correlates very highly with the independently achieved SD scale value of that item.

For many MMPI workers, the continued demonstrations by Edwards and his co-workers have not seemed compelling. Resistance to acceptance of the SD interpretation has been based in part on preferences ingrained by tradition and in part on the stubborn argument that the SD interpretation, although perhaps compatible with earlier established findings, does not lead to new knowledge. However, reluctance to adopt the SD concept should be supported by more than inertia or discontent. Rather, empirical and conceptual analyses are required to evaluate the special contribution of the social desirability interpretation.

We shall now consider the two main sources of support for the SD interpretation to see whether there is a basis for skepticism about the role of SD in determining and distorting MMPI-scale scores. We shall then broaden our argument to evaluate the heuristic value and parsimony of the social desirability concept in the larger realms of personality psychology.

CORRELATES OF THE *SD* SCALE AND THE SOCIAL DESIRABILITY HYPOTHESIS

The impressively high correlations of Edwards' *SD* scale with other MMPI scales have been demonstrated time and again. From the pattern of these correlations, Edwards has argued quite skillfully in support of the *SD* scale as an able measure of the first, and dominant, factor underlying MMPI scales, defending this interpretation against alternative views in terms of content (Edwards & Heathers, 1962) and acquiescence (Edwards & Walker, 1961a; 1961b). The factor structures reported in Chapter

4 are consonant with the factor structures found elsewhere, and it would seem beyond dispute now to deny that the *SD* scale is tantamount to a defining measure of what we noncommittally have been calling the Alpha factor of the MMPI. The question that still must be considered is: What is the special evidence justifying a social desirability interpretation above other interpretations of Alpha that may be raised?

We may dismiss at the outset the suggestion of a priority for the SD interpretation because the *SD* scale can be employed as a "short form" of the MMPI. To the extent that the *SD* scale is presented as such a "short form," measurement of at least the second MMPI dimension will be completely neglected since the *SD* scale is uncorrelated with the sizable Beta component which is shown in Chapter 8 to have many and significant behavioral correlates. The Edwards and Walker demonstration (1961c) that the *SD* scale could function as a short form of the MMPI has equivocal import since the particular MMPI scales the *SD* scores were able to predict were not identified. If the demonstration was conducted with a preponderance of scales loading heavily on the first MMPI factor, then the Edwards and Walker results follow quite readily. But if MMPI scales having zero or small loadings on the first MMPI factor were to be employed, the *SD* scale could have no predictive utility. Thus, the Edwards and Walker result may be seen as a further expression of the pervasiveness of the Alpha dimension within the MMPI but not as specific evidence for the SD interpretation. The MMPI *Pt* scale could have performed as well as the *SD* scale in these analyses since it is an equally excellent measure of the Alpha factor.

It seems fair to conclude, from the body of Edwards' writings, that the essential evidence for interpreting the Alpha dimension in terms of social desirability is simply that the *SD* scale has exceedingly high loadings on this factor. This brings us to consider the construction and characteristics of the *SD* scale.

In developing the *SD* scale, Edwards provided a set of 10 judges with a preselected set of 150 MMPI items, asking them to "role-play" and respond to the items in a socially desirable way. For 79 of the 150 statements, he found perfect agreement among the judges as to the socially desirable response. By a later item-analytic procedure, these 79 items were reduced to the 39 item *SD* scale commonly used by Edwards and others.

Now, the 150 MMPI items presented to the judges for simulated response were not a random selection from the 566 MMPI items available but rather consisted of the items constituting the Taylor Manifest Anxiety (*TMA*) scale (Taylor, 1953), the *F* scale, the *L* scale and the *K* scale. Edwards suggests (1957, p. 29) that this set of items is heterogeneous in content. However—and here lies a basis for irretrievably subverting the *SD* scale and all the relationships it integrates—it can be argued that the preselected pool of 150 items in fact contained narrowly oriented content homogeneities that shaped the composition of the ultimate *SD* scale and built-in the relationships later observed.

An MMPI-sophisticated clinician would judge the content of the item pool used by Edwards as heavily representing that syndrome of personal vulnerability, bodily tension, and unhappiness which may be labeled something akin to susceptibility to anxiety. For our purposes here we need not become especially involved with the concept of anxiety. Although imperfectly defined and understood, there appears to be little disagreement about the core meaning of anxiety and some of its behavioral referents.

Given its starting point, no surprise is occasioned when the *content* of the items constituting the *SD* scale portrays a picture of a personally comfortable individual when the items are responded to in the keyed direction and a description of a chronically tense and anxious person when socially undesirable responses are selected.

Witness the following rather typical items (every sixth one) of the *SD* scale:

43. My sleep is fitful and disturbed (false).
158. I cry easily (false).
241. I dream frequently about things that are best kept to myself (false).
267. When in a group of people I have trouble thinking of the right things to talk about (false).
337. I feel anxiety about something or someone almost all the time (false).
439. It makes me nervous to have to wait (false).

To respond affirmatively to the above set of items is to respond in the socially undesirable direction. At the same time, however, to respond affirmatively is to acknowledge a personal life less satisfying than the respondent desires. Why does he do so? Could socially undesirable responses to these items perhaps be genuine expressions of a subject's inner state?

The subject who responds negatively to the above items responds in the SD way. But does such a pattern of response necessarily signify distortion or could this subject be in fact an individual who sleeps well; is not hyperemotional; does not have disturbing dreams; has a modicum of poise; is not troubled by a vague, incessant uneasiness and portents of doom; and remains relaxed when his expected schedule goes awry? Solely correlational analysis, unassisted by efforts to unconfound or by referral to external behaviors and criteria, cannot discriminate between these conflicting interpretations.

In the meanwhile, however, the content homogeneity of the SD scale permits us to suggest why, on a psychometric basis, the SD scale correlates so highly with the Pt scale and other measures strongly related to the first MMPI factor. We note first that in the 39 item SD scale, 22 of the TMA items—all scored in the opposite direction—are to be found. Because of the extensive item overlap between the SD and TMA scales, these two scales cannot correlate less negatively than about −.7! The TMA scale is well known as an alternative form of the earlier and differently established Pt scale (cf., Brackbill & Little, 1954), correlating—in part because of item overlap—well over .9 with the Pt scale in numerous samples. Hence, the SD scale *must* correlate highly negatively with the Pt scale, as indeed it does in the present and many other analyses. When it is further recognized that Pt is a pure and excellent measure of the Alpha MMPI factor, the sequence by which the SD scale has come to "explain" the Alpha dimension may be understood. But if the Pt scale and Alpha factor are said to be explainable in terms of the SD scale, then equally, the SD scale may be said to be understandable in terms of the Pt scale and Alpha.

The criticism of confounding is a blade that, if held too tightly, will cut its wielder. With the same logic advanced for social desirability as underlying Alpha-related MMPI scales, one can argue that the Alpha factor of the MMPI represents a personality dimension that is vital to an understanding of the *SD* scale. Many of the Alpha-related MMPI scales have empirical origins and demonstrable validity in separating appropriate criterion groups. The high correlations found between these scales and the SD measure therefore plausibly suggest—not an artifact or naïvete in the construction of these earlier scales—but rather that the *SD* scale, wittingly or not, is an excellent measure of some important variable of personality.

It is not difficult to explain how a scale designed to measure social desirability can prove to relate in significant ways to scales developed for comparison, say, of neurotic and nonneurotic groups. If one presumes that, by and large, subjects will respond to the MMPI in a responsible fashion when the test is presented to them as a meaningful task, a high score on, for example, the *Pt* scale will entail a low score on the SD measure because *the signs and symptoms of neuroticism are themselves usually socially undesirable.* This simple, almost patent observation generalizes to all forms of psychopathology—personal maladjustment will tend to generate feelings, attitudes, and behaviors upon which, when judged separately, society generally will frown. The suggestion of a concomitant but not intrinsic relationship between personality and the separate, subsequent evaluation of the behaviors emitted by that personality applies as well to socially valued syndromes —the signs and symptoms of intellectual efficiency, of leadership, or of social participativeness are themselves usually judged as socially desirable. Especially to be noted is the profound difficulty of separating, *a priori,* the specifics of a mode of adjustment from a judgment of that mode's level of social desirability. As an exercise, the reader should attempt to list manifestations of neuroticism that will not be evaluated as socially undesirable.

Edwards has acknowledged the likelihood of an intrinsic relationship between the expressions of certain personality dimensions and social desirability (1957, p. 86) but has chosen to see the SD side of the coin. An MMPI traditionalist can argue with equal plausibility, however, that characterological variables are paramount in the MMPI and that the MMPI correlates of the *SD* scale are fully expectable and of epiphenomenal interest. For him, it is not surprising that the behaviors and feelings acknowledged by a schizophrenic are evaluated in a societal context as undesirable. He would also counterclaim that what is neglected by the social desirability preoccupation is the recognition that not all socially undesirable behaviors are schizophrenic—there are different kinds of social undesirability, different forms psychopathology can take, all of which would be judged as socially undesirable. There are also different conceptions of what is socially desirable, a finding that severely complicates application of a uniform notion of SD, as has been the case so far (*cf.*, Messick, 1960).

The question of the primacy and parsimony of these mutually devouring interpretations cannot be resolved so long as the argument centers around the *SD* scale. The correlates surrounding the *SD* scale, its position as an excellent, but not unique, measure of the Alpha MMPI factor—these observations cannot speak for the necessity of viewing this scale and the underlying factor in social desirability terms because of the intrinsic content linkages of this scale with the other scales it proposes to explain.

To extricate these fused alternatives, two logical possibilities exist. First, a scale measuring SD but one which is not contentually homogenous should be constructed and its relationship to the Alpha dimension explored. I find it difficult to anticipate how such a scale might be developed without a fundamental revision of Edwards' conception of SD.

The second approach is to construct a scale measuring the Alpha factor but one which cannot also be interpreted in SD terms. This latter course is taken and the goal achieved in the next chapter, Chapter 7.

PROPORTION OF ENDORSEMENTS AND SOCIAL DESIRABILITY SCALE VALUE

An early demonstration by Edwards (1953) was that the proportion of individuals in a group answering "true" to an inventory statement is strongly related to the social desirability scale value (SDSV) of the item. That is, for each inventory item the proportion of subjects in the group responding affirmatively is established. Edwards refers to these proportions as probabilities of item endorsement. Separately and independently, the SDSV of each item is obtained. The correlation, across the full set of MMPI items, between the set of proportions and the paired SDSV's is usually in the middle .80's and, on occasion, goes above .90. This relationship has been observed often and is not in dispute.

The question, however, is just what does this relationship signify or necessarily entail? Without explicitly indicating the significance of the phenomenon, Edwards nevertheless conveys the impression that the high correlation between SDSVs and proportions of item endorsement devastates interpreting the individual's response to items in any but SD terms. The problem of understanding is not helped by Edwards' usage of the label, *probability of item endorsement,* when the referent is to the proportion of a group. This label is interpreted as a response tendency existing *within* the individual subject rather than, as is the case, a summary statistic descriptive of a particular group. The importance of this confusion between interpretation and referent stems from the fact that *the relationships characterizing an aggregation of individuals tell little about the relationships existing within an individual.* Group-based proportions are predictive only of other indices describing that or an equivalent aggregation. The distinction between relationships characterizing a group and relationships characterizing an individual is essential to maintain, well-known (*cf.,* Bakan, 1954; Estes, 1956; Mandler, 1959; Sidman, 1952; Thorndike, 1939), and not contested but appears to have had little impact on research designs or orientations toward data analysis.

To exemplify this distinction in the present context, consider that the correlation between "probability of item endorsement" and SDSV is a correlation between two sets of averages—the *average* tendency, expressed in proportion form, of an item to "pull" an endorsement and the *average* SDSV assigned to that item by a set of scalers. The items with the highest proportions of endorsement tend to have the highest SDSVs, as reflected by correlations of .8 or .9 between these two sets of averages.

The controversy surrounding the social desirability interpretation, however, focuses upon the influence of SD within the *individual subject*. What is required is the correlation, for each individual in a sample, between item endorsement and SDSV.
These individual correlations may then in turn be averaged to
provide a fairer summary indication of the relationship as it exists
within the average individual. The correlation of averages is *not*
the same as the average correlation and, on statistical grounds,
we know that the average correlation must be very much lower
than the figures based on grouped data used by Edwards to support the decisiveness of SD.

In addition, it is important to know the *range* of these individual correlations so that the descriptive usefulness of their average
may be assessed. If the individual subjects vary widely in regard
to their tendency to say "true" to items inclined toward SD, then
no summarizing index may be justified and analyses of this differential tendency should study this variable in its full diversity.

Taylor (1959) has studied the relationship of item endorsement to SDSVs for each of 70 male schizophrenics. When the data
were grouped and the averages correlated, the usual high correlation (.79) was obtained between the proportion of endorsements and SDSVs. However, when calculated separately for each
subject, the average point-biserial correlation was only .39. There
was a wide range of variation about this average in Taylor's sample. Taylor also observed—a most important finding—that subjects manifesting psychopathological response to the MMPI were
quite knowledgeable and conventional in their understanding of
the norms of SD. Ignorance of or deviance from normative values
cannot account for the failure to endorse modal responses.

To replicate and extend Taylor's findings in additional samples,
the relationship of item endorsement to SDSV was evaluated in
the present study. For each subject in each of Samples A through
E, the point-biserial correlation was calculated between his
"trues" and "falses" and the SDSVs developed by Messick and
Jackson (1961b). A summary of the results is presented in the
first portion of Table 16.

It will be observed that although again, endorsement proportions based on grouped data correlate highly with SDSVs, the

TABLE 16

The Correlation between Item Endorsement and SD Scale Value as a Function of Grouped versus Individual Data and the Distribution of SD Scale Values

Sample	Correlation based on grouped data and all MMPI items	Mean of individual correlations based on all MMPI items	Range of individual correlations based on all MMPI items	Correlation based on grouped data and normally distributed MMPI items	Mean of individual correlations based on normally distributed MMPI items	Range of individual correlations based on normally distributed MMPI items
A	.82	.57	.30 to .71	.63	.37	.06 to .57
B	.84	.55	.19 to .71	.64	.30	.05 to .60
C	.81	.54	.24 to .69	.56	.30	−.02 to .46
D	.79	.48	.10 to .70	.54	.29	−.02 to .51
E	.78	.49	−.01 to .73	.55	.30	−.19 to .50

average individual correlation between endorsed items and SDSVs is appreciably lower. The *range* of individual correlations in a given sample is especially striking, indicating that even within the framework of the SD hypothesis individuals vary widely with respect to the extent to which they may be said to be influenced by their notions of SD when filling out the MMPI. The use of a solitary coefficient based on grouped data clearly is erroneous in its suggestion as to the potency of SD in influencing item endorsements in the individual case.

Before going on to explore the correlates and possible origin of these individual differences in correlations between endorsement and SDSV, it is necessary to assure ourselves that these individual differences do in fact reliably exist and that no way of assimilating these findings to earlier interpretations may be found. Certain statistical considerations that conceivably might be called into play as potential explanations of the low individual correlations and their range must be evaluated to see whether they can subsume the discrepancies observed between the individual and grouped data. This problem must be worried because the correlation coefficient manifests various vagaries in this special context that limit its usefulness qua correlation coefficient and because the correspondence between item endorsement and SDSV has been a primary basis of the SD interpretation of the MMPI and analogous item pools.

The three statistical matters to be taken up are: (1) the effects of attenuation in producing discrepancies between data at the individual and grouped levels; (2) certain deficiencies in the point-biserial coefficient vis-à-vis the product-moment correlation calculated from continua; and (3) the influence of the distributional form of SDSVs in determining the magnitude of the correlations observed. The first of these proves to be insignificant in effect, the second operates unfairly *against* the SD hypothesis, while the last works unfairly *for* the SD interpretation. On balance, we believe our results stand and that earlier inferences drawn about the overall and impressive potency of SD in influencing item endorsement were misleading. The reader not requiring the convoluted details surrounding this conclusion may accept it on faith and omit the next several pages, going on to the discussion of how the sometime relationships in the individual between endorsement and SDSV can originate on different grounds.

First, consider the possibility that the unreliability of an individual's item endorsement will attenuate the relationship between endorsement and SD scale values within that subject. We know that grouping provides highly reliable data. Can it be that the appreciably lower relationships observed at the individual level are due to the subject's response unreliability? To respond to this question, information on the test-retest stability of item endorsement is required. Goldberg and Rorer (1963) have reported such data, based on a sample of 95 college males and another sample of 108 college females. Intervals of four weeks separated the two MMPI administrations. Enough time elapsed and there were enough items so that specific memory of earlier responses is not a significant factor. The average percentage consistency of response over all MMPI items was .83 and .87, respectively, for the two samples studied. Of the 203 subjects only one showed less than 77% response consistency (Rorer, 1964). In another, earlier study, Schofield (1948) found equivalent results. Given these high figures and the narrow range of individual differences, and when it is further recognized that a number of the MMPI items are "mood" items especially susceptible to temporal excursions, the consistency of responses to the MMPI is indeed impressive. If these several results are typical—and there is no reason for presuming otherwise—there is an insufficient basis for invoking an attenuation explanation of the lower individual correlations of item endorsement with SD scale values.

A second concern to note is the unsatisfactory statistical nature of the point-biserial correlation coefficient in the present application. Point-biserial *rs*, although product-moment coefficients, fall on a more compressed scale than product-moment *rs* based solely on continuous variables—they cannot attain values of 1.00 even when a perfect relationship exists. Moreover, biserial coefficients are further lowered as an individual's proportions of "trues" and "falses" deviates from 50-50. These deficiencies of the point-biserial coefficient obviously operate to lower unfairly the relationship between item endorsement and SD scale values when considered at the individual level and are sufficient, conjoined with even a minimal attenuation effect, to explain a sizable portion of the discrepancy between the correlation of group-based averages (where continua are involved) and the average biserial correlation (where a dichotomy is employed). The matter cannot be left here, however, without considering a previously unnoted factor operating to exaggerate the relationship found between item endorsement and SD scale values.

The distribution of SD scale values using either the Messick and Jackson or the Heineman entries is severely bimodal, the modes being positioned near the two ends of the continuum with emphasis especially on the undesirable end of the distribution. Now the nature of the product-moment correlation, in either its continuous or biserial forms, is that elements are weighted as an inverse squared function of their distance from the mean of the distribution. When correlating distributions, one or both of which are bimodal, the coefficients obtained move toward the extremes of ±1.00. This accentuation of correlations as a function of bimodality can be very striking.

Obviously, the particular shape of the distribution of SDSVs for the full set of MMPI items is arbitrary and accidental. It readily could have been changed at the time of item selection if foreseen as a problem. However, given the specific and express orientation of the item pool toward psychiatric diagnosis, Hathaway and his co-workers might well have chosen to maintain the item pool unchanged on the grounds that the diagnostic validity of the inventory might be lowered by reshaping items to conform to the distributional needs of a particular correlation coefficient.

One way of assessing the contribution of the bimodality effect to the correlations found between item endorsement and SDSV is to determine the correlations resulting if an MMPI-item pool with a normal distribution of SDSVs is employed. A normal distribution is not a prerequisite for calculating a correlation coefficient; its usage is suggested simply because unimodal distributions reasonably close to normality are conventional or usual in psychology. To show the influence of bimodality on the magnitude of the correlations obtained, comparison with a reference distribution is required and the normal distribution is an obvious anchoring choice.

The MMPI-item pool cannot be revised in any genuine way to comport with these belated requirements; but as an indication of what would result if a normal distribution of SDSVs obtained for the MMPI, it is reasonable to shave the existing distribution into a normal form by deleting—on a random basis—items with SDSVs of excessive frequency. Accordingly, a 21 interval normal distribution was imposed upon the distribution of Messick and Jackson SDSVs, centered at the scaling midpoint, with an ordinate set to maximize the number of items in the central interval. Within these constraints and employing a random exclusion method, it proved necessary to drop 360 of the 566 MMPI items in order to conform to the normal distribution—testimony to the degree of bimodality present in the full MMPI.

Now, the remaining 206 items may be thought of as an MMPI-item pool equivalent on a sampling basis to the original pool except for the distribution of SDSVs. The effect of the shape of this distribution now can be assessed by correlating item endorsements with SDSVs for this reduced set of items. The results of these analyses for Sample A through E may be read from the last three columns of Table 16 where it will be noted that the bimodality effect in the full MMPI has powerfully enhanced correlations beyond the values achieved within a normal distribution. The amount of variance "explainable" by the bimodally-based correlations is about halved when a normal distribution is employed. Thus, the seeming influence of SD on item endorsement, as reflected by the absolute magnitude of the correlations between endorsement and SDSV, is an arbitrary function of the shape of the SDSV distribution employed. Clearly, a more invariant and supportable index is required.

The foregoing analyses and statistical discussion have indicated it is unprofitable in the interpretive dispute to dwell on the absolute and arbitrary magnitude of correlations between item endorsement and SDSV. The net resultant of conjoining attenuation, point-biserial deficiencies, and the shape of the distributions of SDSVs is unknown and, happily, this information is unimportant because *the range of individual correlations is essentially unaffected by these considerations.* Some respondents tend to say "true" to the items keyed for SD in the MMPI, and some do not.

The extent of these indisputable individual differences augurs and argues for a rather different state of affairs than is suggested by focusing on a solitary coefficient based on or referred to the relation between sets of averages. Let us proceed now to some reasoning and analyses designed to place in different perspective the relationship of endorsement and SDSV within and between responding subjects.

It will be shown that the variable tendency in individuals to endorse SD-keyed responses is a further reflection of certain structural characteristics of the MMPI-item pool, in particular, the excessive specification of the first or Alpha factor. Earlier in this chapter, it was contended that an SD interpretation of the first MMPI factor has by no means yet excluded other conceptual explanations. Accordingly, a demonstration that endorsement-SDSV correlations are an entailed manifestation of the Alpha dimension is *not* additional or convergent evidence for the SD hypothesis— the Alpha dimension must earn its interpretation from unconfounding analyses and on independent grounds. In support of this generally-stated reinterpretation, consider the following chain of argument and some attendant relationships.

At the individual level, the correlation between item endorsement and SDSV may be taken as a "score" or index. For convenience, we shall label this set of individual correlations as the Desirability-Correlated Response variable (DCR). For some individuals, the DCR score is moderately high signifying that SD— whether causally or epiphenomenally—is involved in determining specific responses; in other subjects, the DCR index is low or even negative, suggesting response is determined alternatively.

The correlation of the DCR variable with the Alpha dimension is quite high. For example, in Samples A through E, DCR correlates with the *SD* scale: .82, .75, .78, .90, and .90. The correlations of the DCR with other good measures of Alpha, such as the *Pt* scale, are of equal magnitude. It appears, then, that DCR scores (*i.e.*, individual correlations between item endorsement and SDSV) are a good substitute for scores on the Alpha continuum. Why should this be so?

In Chapter 5, it was demonstrated that the Alpha dimension is vastly represented within the MMPI-item pool. It was further noted that with rare exceptions, the Alpha-related items were located toward the one or the other end of the SD scaling continuum. Because of this confounding, a subject responding strictly in terms of an SD orientation would endorse and deny items according to their SD keying but, at the same time, a subject responding consistently to Alpha items on a more differentiated and psychological basis would, inescapably, prove also to have aligned his responses with SDSVs. This ever present and pervasive confounding, built-in when the MMPI-item pool was selected, permits the range of DCR individual differences to be understood either in terms of SD or in terms of a non-SD interpretation of Alpha. There are no grounds, within these data, for a choice between these alternatives.

By way of further relationships concordant with the view that DCR scores are determined by intrinsic or "method" (Wiggins, 1962) characteristics of the MMPI, recall that there is an imbalance in the keying of Alpha-relevant items, only about one-quarter of them being keyed for "true." As we have seen, this asymmetry in the direction of item writing accounted for the possibility of an acquiescence interpretation in the absence of more complete knowledge. It follows from this imbalance that an inverse relationship should exist between an individual's frequency of item endorsement and his DCR or SD score. Within the MMPI, because of its structural emphases, the greater the number of items endorsed by a subject, the less his tendency to restrict endorsement solely to Alpha-positive items. And by endorsing Alpha-negative items, an individual's DCR or SD score will be decreased.

This expectation is based solely on knowledge of fortuitous properties of the MMPI. Regrettably for the chances of a critical confrontation, the SD interpretation can generate the equivalent prediction because it is well known that socially undesirable items predominate in the MMPI. Consequently, increasing the number of endorsed items will necessarily begin to involve affirmation of undesirable statements.

Whatever the basis of extrapolation, the prediction proves valid and the results are of interest in their own right. The correlations of proportion of items endorsed by an individual with his

DCR score, for Samples A through E are: —.47, —.38, —.41, —.63, and —.63. The correlations of proportions of items endorsed with SD scores are, for the five samples: —.61, —.47, —.58, —.75, and —.65. The highest correspondences between item endorsement and SDSV (and the highest SD scores) tend to occur in subjects endorsing rather few items (endorsement proportions in the range of .26 to .32); the lowest DCR (and SD) scores go along with a more frequent affirmation of MMPI items (endorsment proportions in the vicinity of .50 to .60). Thus, it may be seen again that the range of individual correlations between endorsement and SDSV, although compatible with the SD position, may be derived as well from the pattern of representation of a non-SD dimension within the item pool.

In summary of this section on the significance of the correspondence between item endorsement and SDSV, which has been heavily emphasized as a fundamental support of the SD interpretation, it has been argued that this correspondence properly can only be viewed at the individual level and not on the group level, as before. And, at the individual level, this correspondence proves to be highly variable and at most only moderate. Such correspondence as does exist may be fully explained as a function of some intrinsic but essentially accidental facets of the MMPI-item pool. Because the degree of correspondence between item endorsement and SDSV in individuals may be seen to derive from the primacy of the Alpha dimension within the MMPI, these correspondences provide no independent or special support for the SD interpretation of Alpha over competitive interpretations. Judged strictly from this data basis, the interpretive issue remains obscure.

THE HEURISTIC VALUE OF THE SOCIAL DESIRABILITY HYPOTHESIS

One way of evaluating the relative significance of the characterological and social desirability interpretations is to shift to a question of a different order: After departing from the realm of personality inventories, what are the conceptual properties and predictive power of these competing notions?

Posing the issue in this form is perhaps somewhat unfair to the SD viewpoint in that applications of the concept to behavioral settings have not been fully developed. Edwards has suggested, however, that "differences in the behavior of high and low scoring groups (on the SD dimension) will be found in those situations where the behavior under study has itself a large proportion of its variance in common with the social desirability variable" (1957, p. 91). He indicates that learning tasks and other behaviors influenced by the motivation to look good are likely to be understandable in SD terms.

As a specific application of this predictive possibility, he cites some of the research relating the *TMA* scale to learning efficiency. In certain of these studies, it was observed that *TMA* defined "anxious" individuals performed less well in learning situations than did "nonanxious" subjects. Since the *TMA* scale is strongly related, inversely, to the *SD* scale, Edwards hypothesizes that the "nonanxious" subjects in these studies may be viewed as interested in making a good impression (*i.e.*, they have strong SDRTs) and the anxious subjects as having weak SDRTs. In learning tasks, fast learning is socially desirable and so the group with greater SDRTs may be hypothesized to perform better.

This expectation fails to hold water. To some extent, the prediction of Edwards appears to have some empirical support but only when *complex* learning tasks are at issue. When *simple* learning tasks are employed the relationships observed appear to reverse—subjects who are "anxious" (and have weak SDRTs) learn faster than subjects who are "nonanxious" (and have strong SDRTs). It is difficult to see how this interaction between SDRT and the simplicity-complexity of learning tasks can be reconciled with the SD hypothesis. Taylor (1956) and Sarason (1960) have summarized many of the relevant studies and provide an integration of the diverse findings by theoretical orientations that continue or reinstate the anxiety concept as fundamentally required. A direct analysis of the relationship of SD to learning is provided by Stricker (1963) who concludes that inordinate complications surround usage of the SD hypothesis to explain the patchy results obtained.

Edwards apparently has not gone beyond this extrapolation to the noninventory world, and we are left with the task of inferring from the definition and connotations of the concept just what the behavioral referents of the SDRT (our Alpha dimension) might be. The SD formulation would appear to imply that Alpha Highs are not truly psychologically healthy, but rather, are simulating all social virtues. Similarly, the indications of personal distress endorsed by Alpha Lows should not be taken as serious expressions since these simply are persons who do not have the usually strong SDRT. From this conception, SD-based predictions relating to situations other than self-description tasks are difficult to formulate and it is in this sense that the SD concept is not heuristic. Yet it is in the direction of generalization of the applicability of concepts that psychology must go.

As we have seen, within the MMPI, Edwards rejects a characterological interpretation of Alpha as unclarifying because it invokes inferential constructs or hazily evolved notions which often are not well delineated. The SD concept, on the other hand, pridefully denies any surplus meaning—it is what it is. Even though, as we have argued, the *SD* scale is an equivocal instrument, its ubiquitous correlations within the MMPI together with the simplicity of the SD notion can make this interpretation an appealing and parsimonious one so long as inquiry is restricted to correlational analyses of MMPI scales.

But when the first MMPI factor is related to behavior beyond the MMPI, the SD concept appears to falter and a more theoretical approach *can* come into its own. We must see whether a characterological interpretation of Alpha *does* become regnant when the view of behavior is broadened, whether essentially the same psychodynamic constructs previously put forward to identify the Alpha factor continue to apply in other behavioral contexts. A conceptual congruence across data domains, if established, provides a higher order of understanding. Moreover, as a result of this reciprocal understanding, the constructs being employed become less abstruse and tenuous. In Chapter 8 some evidence is presented testifying to the fruitfulness and economy of a psychodynamic interpretation of the Alpha dimension as judged from non-MMPI behaviors. Until the reader arrives at these results and their persuasiveness is evaluated, our argument is only provisional. The social desirability concept presently appears to have little predictive or integrative value in the larger context of personality measurement and personality research. Characterological concepts, on the other hand, have the promise of reaching beyond the inventory world and of achieving parsimony at a *conceptual* level.

7

DEVELOPING A DESIRABILITY-FREE MEASURE OF "SOCIAL DESIRABILITY"

In this chapter, we describe the construction of a scale to measure the Alpha factor of the MMPI, the factor for which Edwards has proposed an interpretation in terms of social desirability. Although excellent measures of the Alpha dimension exist (*e.g., SD, Pt*), the dilemma posed by these scales is that they may be interpreted from either a characterological or a SD standpoint. The Alpha-measuring scale to be described and then evaluated measures the first factor of the MMPI exceedingly well but has been constructed so as to be "desirability-free." A scale that identifies the Alpha dimension although fairly excluding the influence of SD clarifies a formerly muddled situation since a "desirability-free" measure of Alpha is an untenable anomaly, given the SD hypothesis. It can arise if—and only if—the Alpha factor is a dimension thus far fortuitously linked to SD but not necessarily so. If the Alpha factor of the MMPI can be well measured without invoking the SD concept, then it follows that the SD interpretation does not intrinsically apply in this context.

Our strategy in the construction of this scale was to select Alpha-related items which concomitantly are neutral with respect to SD or are even keyed against the SD hypothesis. It proved possible to choose items meeting these dual criteria within the MMPI by virtue of some earlier analyses and a vast redundancy in representation of the Alpha factor.

It will be recalled, from Chapter 5, that in studying the proper-

ties of the MMPI-item pool, an item analysis was performed
using as contrast groups the Alpha Highs (combined from Samples A through E, providing a total N of 95) and the Alpha Lows
(combined from all 5 samples, the total N being 97). The three
samples of men were combined with the two samples of women
because separate analyses for the sexes indicated that with respect to the Alpha dimension, there were no distinguishable
differences between men and women in regard to the psychological content of Alpha-discriminating items.

In these analyses of combined subgroups, 389 of the 566 MMPI
items (68.7%) proved to discriminate at the .10 level of significance. At the .05 level, the figure was 355 items (62.7%) and at
the .01 level, 292 items (51.6%). These are spectacular findings
and testify to the extent of repetition within the MMPI-item pool
of Alpha-relevant items. Because of the large sizes of the contrast
groups employed, these figures, although still lower bounds,
probably come close to the limiting (*i.e.*, true) values.

Of the 389 items significant at the .10 level, 109 items (28%)
are answered more affirmatively by the high scorers on the Alpha
dimension and 280 items (72%) are responded to more frequently
by low scoring individuals. As indexed by the SD scale values for
MMPI items reported by Messick and Jackson (1961) or by
Heineman (1952), the vast preponderance of the differentiating
items are at one extreme of the SD continuum or the other. The
items affirmed by Alpha Highs tend to be socially desirable; the
items affirmed by Alpha Lows tend to be socially undesirable.

But—and here is the potential we have tapped—there are a
number of MMPI items significantly associated with the first
MMPI factor which are in the neutral ranges of the SD continuum or even on the atypical side—given the particular contrast
group—of the SD dimension. A scale comprised of such SD-
neutral or SD-reverse-keyed Alpha items should measure the first
factor of the MMPI but should not be vulnerable to an interpretation in terms of SD. As a matter of esthetic nicety but, as we
have seen, by no means required, such a desirability-free Alpha
scale should be constructed to have as many items keyed for a
"true" response as are keyed for a "false" response, thus eliminating the intrusion (of the interpretation) of a possible acquiescence-response set.

Obviously, the logic of this approach depends on, besides the availability of a horde of Alpha-related items, an acceptable basis for identifying the scale position of these items on the SD continuum. Unless the SD scale values (SDSVs) of the items selected to constitute the proposed scale are recognized as meeting the promised criteria, the scale and its correlates would roil instead of calm the contentious atmosphere.

The two most widely used and publicly available sets of SDSVs for the MMPI-item pool are those of Heineman (1952, reported also in Dahlstrom & Welsh, 1960) and Messick and Jackson (1961b). The Heineman scale values were developed using 108 college students as judges, a 5-point rating scale, and the method of equal-appearing intervals. The rating variabilities for each item are not published. The Messick and Jackson SDSVs were established employing 171 judges, a 9-point rating scale, and the method of successive intervals. Rating dispersions for each item were calculated. Messick and Jackson report a correlation of .964 between their scale values and those obtained by Heineman.

With the advent of the Messick and Jackson scale values, there has been a shift toward their use over the Heineman results, where such information is required. The grounds for this preference are multiple and cumulative: the Messick and Jackson results are more recent; a larger judge sample was used; finer discriminations are available; the scaling method employed was more sophisticated; and the additional, useful information about item-rating dispersions (*i.e.*, item ambiguity) is available. Accordingly, in specifying the SDSVs of the Alpha-related items, the Messick and Jackson results were used.

A total of 40 items were selected according to the criteria and are defined as the *Ego-Resiliency* (*Subtle*) or *ER-S* scale. The label assigned to this scale is believed to follow from the behavioral correlates of the Alpha dimension, reported in the next chapter. The *ER-S* scale consists of 20 items scored in the "true" direction and 20 items scored in the "false" direction. Each subset of 20 items contains items chosen almost exclusively from the middle intervals of the SD scaling continuum, and the two subsets have equivalent SDSV means and standard deviations. For the 20 items keyed "true," the mean SDSV is 5.11, with a standard deviation of

.64; for the 20 items keyed "false," the mean SDSV is 5.21, with a standard deviation of .62. Moreover, the rating dispersions of the selected items are not unusual. For the 20 items keyed "true," the mean rating dispersion is 1.72; for the 20 items keyed "false," the mean rating dispersion is 1.48; the overall mean dispersion being 1.60. These figures may be compared with the mean rating dispersion of 1.64 based on the 40 MMPI items: 1, 51, 101, . . . 551,2, 52, 102, etc. At the .01 level of significance, 36 of the ER-S items were related to the Alpha dimension. Of the remaining 4 items, all in the "true" subscale, 3 were Alpha-significant at the .05 level and 1 at the .10 level.

By virtue of the dual criteria employed in assembling items, we suggest that neither a "yea-sayer" nor an individual who responds in a socially desirable way can earn an extreme score on the full *ER-S* scale. The items defining the *ER-S* scale are reported in Table 17.

Edwards (1962) has maintained that scores achieved on the *ER-S* scale could still be influenced by the SD response set. He has observed that, if the Heineman scale values are employed to assess SD, instead of the Messick and Jackson values, the 72% instead of 50% of the items in the *ER-S* scale turn out to be keyed for socially desirable responses. As a corollary, the "true"-keyed items in the *ER-S* scale are on the average, .4 of an interval more socially desirable than the "false"-keyed items, when judged by the Heineman standards (2.58 versus 2.98).

This criticism of the *ER-S* scale depends on rejection of the Messick and Jackson SD scale values which, in other contexts, Edwards appears to prefer (Edwards, Diers, & Walker, 1962; Edwards, Gocka, & Holloway, 1963; Edwards & Walsh, 1963.) It further depends on *dichotomous* identification of items as keyed in the SD direction or not, using the nominal neutral point as the basis for categorization. In the construction of the *ER-S* scale, the *intensity* of the SD keying was respected because it was believed that such *continuous* keying would improve upon the gross index afforded by dichotomous keying. The logical refinement of intensity keying has been justified empirically by Edwards and Walsh (1963).

Although Edwards' interpositions are themselves debatable, an

TABLE 17
The Items Defining the MMPI *ER-S* Scale

Item No.	Item Text	Scoring Direction	Messick and Jackson SDSV
36.	I seldom worry about my health.	True	5.29
68.	I hardly ever feel pain in the back of the neck.	True	5.64
73.	I am an important person.	True	4.19
74.	I have often wished I were a girl. (Or if you are a girl) I have never been sorry that I am a girl.	True	4.57
91.	I do not mind being made fun of.	True	5.19
119.	My speech is the same as always (not faster or slower, or slurring; no hoarseness).	True	5.45
131.	I do not worry about catching diseases.	True	5.62
167.	It wouldn't make me nervous if any members of my family got into trouble with the law.	True	3.34
198.	I daydream very little.	True	5.60
222.	It is not hard for me to ask help from my friends even though I cannot return the favor.	True	4.66
235.	I have been quite independent and free from family rule.	True	5.19
242.	I believe I am no more nervous than most others.	True	5.82
270.	When I leave home I do not worry about whether the door is locked and the windows closed.	True	4.48
306.	I get all the sympathy I should.	True	5.10
329.	I almost never dream.	True	4.71
369.	Religion gives me no worry.	True	5.45
478.	I have never been made especially nervous over trouble that any members of my family have gotten into.	True	4.57
523.	I practically never blush.	True	5.68
528.	I blush no more often than others.	True	5.79
532.	I can stand as much pain as others can.	True	5.85
5.	I am easily awakened by noise.	False	4.34
71.	I think a great many people exaggerate their misfortunes in order to gain the sympathy and help of others.	False	4.84

TABLE 17 (*Continued*)

Item No.	Item Text	Scoring Direction	Messick and Jackson SDSV
89.	It takes a lot of argument to convince most people of the truth.	False	4.84
102.	My hardest battles are with myself.	False	4.99
112.	I frequently find it necessary to stand up for what I think is right.	False	7.50
134.	At times my thoughts have raced ahead faster than I could speak them.	False	5.51
201.	I wish I were not so shy.	False	5.47
279.	I drink an unusually large amount of water every day.	False	4.75
323.	I have had very peculiar and strange experiences.	False	5.10
327.	My mother or father often made me obey even when I thought that it was unreasonable.	False	5.11
382.	I wish I could get over worrying about things I have said that may have injured other people's feelings.	False	5.19
390.	I have often felt badly over being misunderstood when trying to keep someone from making a mistake.	False	5.00
394.	I frequently ask people for advice.	False	5.77
402.	I often must sleep over a matter before I decide what to do.	False	5.07
425.	I dream frequently.	False	4.89
458.	The man who had most to do with me when I was a child (such as my father, stepfather, etc.) was very strict with me.	False	5.05
465.	I have several times had a change of heart about my life work.	False	5.19
468.	I am often sorry because I am so cross and grouchy.	False	5.63
489.	I feel sympathetic toward people who tend to hang on to their griefs and troubles.	False	4.77
505.	I have had periods when I felt so full of pep that sleep did not seem necessary for days at a time.	False	5.18

attempt was made to assimilate these objections by revising the *ER-S* scale. In what follows, it must be kept in mind that on the 9-point scale employed by Messick and Jackson, *high* values indicate SD; on the 5-point continuum used by Heineman, *low* values indicate SD.

By eliminating 12 items from the *ER-S* scale, the remaining 28 items constitute a scale that meets Edwards' suggestion with regard to the Heineman scale values. The 12 items to be eliminated from the *ER-S* scale are the following: keyed "true"— 68, 131, 242, 306, 528, and 532; keyed "false"—5, 71, 323, 425, 458, and 489. The 28 items, dubbed the *ER-SH1* scale, now balance with respect to Heineman scale values (the "true" subscale has a mean Heineman scale value of 2.77 and the "false" subscale a mean of 2.81), but the scale is awry with respect to Messick and Jackson scale values ("true" and "false" subscale means of 4.88 and 5.37, respectively) tending to be keyed *against* SD when judged in terms of the latter values. This 28-item scale still does not meet the dichotomous keying criteria of Edwards, being keyed 17-11 in the SD direction. Dropping a further 8 items (items 36, 91, 369, and 523, all keyed "true;" and items 89, 279, 390, and 505, all keyed "false") finally produces a scale, labeled *ER-SH2*, which has as many items dichotomously-keyed for SD as are dichotomously-keyed against SD. This 20-item scale, however, is now by both sets of SD scale values intensity-keyed against SD. The "true" and "false" subscale means, according to the Messick and Jackson scale values, are 4.68 and 5.54, respectively; using the Heineman values, these figures are 2.91 and 2.67.

This juggling of item-selection criteria introduces new facets of difference and noncomparability while lowering scale reliability because of scale shortening. In another, less constraining item pool, perhaps these several conflicting criteria can be served. In the present, less than optimal circumstance, shortening the *ER-S* scale to 28- or 20-item versions probably is not worth the bother as it does not produce significant differences. By virtue of item overlap alone—overlap which in this situation represents no artifact—the *ER-S* scale will correlate no lower than .83 with *ER-SH1* and no lower than .71 with *ER-SH2*. In fact, the correlations are appreciably higher than these lower bounds. In nine separate samples, the average correlation between ER-S and ER-SH1 is .94; the average correlation between ER-S and ER-SH2 is .88. Because of this correlational comparability, and because of a preference for the Messick and Jackson SDSVs and intensity keying, and because of its higher reliability, we have chosen to continue with the 40-item ER-S scale, evaluating only its properties in this monograph.

In Table 18 are presented the means, standard deviations, and Kuder-Richardson Formula 20 reliabilities of the ER-S scale, for nine different samples. Samples A through E have been previously described (see Chapter 4) and, when combined, formed the basis for the item analysis from which the ER-S items were selected. Samples F through I are additional samples employed to extend our knowledge of the functioning of the ER-S scale in samples fully independent of the scale's development. These latter samples may be briefly characterized:

Sample F consisted of 154 United States Marines, composed in about equal parts of recruits awaiting discharge because of their homosexual tendencies, recruits awaiting discharge for psychiatric reasons (but excluding homosexual involvement), and recruits satisfactorily completing their initial period of training. Sample F was a peculiar mélange, representing psychological disturbance more than psychological health.

Sample G contained 79 women seen at clinics of a university medical center. About half of this group were hypertensives, the remainder being clinic patients matched with the first half on a variety of nonmedical criteria.

Sample H consisted of 76 college women, half of them being defined as prehypertensive because of blood pressure liability and the remainder being matched with the first 38 subjects on a variety of nonphysiological criteria.

Sample I consisted of 87 female clinic patients, about half being hypertensive and the remainder being controls. The primary difference between Sample I and Sample G is that Sample I was collected more recently.

It will be seen from Table 18 that the ER-S scale enjoys adequate but not superb reliability. Samples A through E average a reliability slightly higher than the average earned by Samples F

TABLE 18
Descriptive Statistics for the *ER-S*, *SD* and *Pt* MMPI Scales in Nine Different Samples

Sample	ER-S Scale (40 items)			SD Scale (39 items)			ER-S/SD cor.	ER-S/SD cor., adj.	Pt Scale (48 items)			ER-S/Pt cor.	ER-S/Pt cor., adj.
	Mean	S.D.	K-R 20 rel.	Mean	S.D.	K-R 20 rel.			Mean	S.D.	K-R 20 rel.		
A	25.63	4.79	.704	34.89	3.22	.700	.698	.994	6.53	4.93	.810	−.795	−1.00
B	24.84	5.60	.775	34.01	3.85	.756	.701	.916	7.53	5.03	.801	−.752	−.954
C	24.52	4.27	.610	33.37	4.23	.790	.641	.923	9.07	5.72	.833	−.665	−.933
D	23.81	5.82	.781	31.16	5.31	.831	.765	.950	10.81	7.28	.884	−.792	−.953
E	23.27	5.36	.741	30.80	5.94	.864	.793	.991	12.51	8.25	.906	−.791	−.965
F	18.26	5.08	.674	22.56	7.96	.886	.638	.773	23.80	11.17	.929	−.673	−.851
G	21.18	4.31	.561	27.73	5.39	.792	.671	1.000	15.30	8.36	.888	−.658	−.932
H	23.08	4.82	.674	30.70	4.71	.759	.655	.916	12.17	6.22	.819	−.699	−.941
I	19.55	4.53	.609	26.51	5.76	.811	.592	.842	17.97	9.08	.902	−.610	−.823

93

through I, a difference probably due to the slight capitalization on chance resulting from applying the *ER-S* scale to samples involved in its construction. But the reliability of the *ER-S* scale, even in totally new samples, is fully in keeping with the reliabilities usually attained by MMPI scales and may be compared with those reported in Table 6. Comparatively, the *ER-S* scale is shorter than many MMPI scales, suggesting that the reliability of the scale might be appreciably increased if more items of the *ER-S* variety could be added. This possibility does not appear to exist within the constraints set by the MMPI-item pool.

It will be recalled from Chapter 4 that both the *SD* and *Pt* scales—the latter reversed—are collinear with the Alpha dimension. Let us see how the *ER-S* scale relates to these two measures. The relevant data are contained in Table 18 where it will be observed that the correlations between *ER-S* and *SD*, and between *ER-S* and *Pt* are extremely high.

Thus, for the nine samples, the correlations between *ER-S* and *SD* were, respectively: .70, .70, .64, .77, .79, .64, .67, .66, and .59. Corrected for the attenuating effects of the unreliabilities involved, these figures zoom to about the correlational limit, *i.e.*, .99, .92, .92, .95, .99, .77, 1.00, .92, and .84. These are impressive correlations and indicate the *ER-S* scale—designed to exclude the influence of a SD response tendency—measures the same dimension indexed by the *SD* scale. That is, the Alpha dimension can be measured with no reference to the SD concept.[17]

---

[17] In order to evaluate Edwards' suggestion that the *ER-S* scale is, according to the Heineman SD scale values, still interpretable in SD terms, the "false" subscale within the *ER-S* scale was also correlated with the *SD* scale. As luck would have it, the 20 items constituting the "false"-scored portion of the *ER-S* scale are, by Heineman standards, only slightly dichotomously-keyed for social desirability (12-8 instead of the ideal 10-10) and are intensity-keyed at dead center (mean SDSV of 2.98). The dichotomous keying imbalance in this subscale clearly is insufficient to determine an appreciable correlation with the *SD* scale. And, it will be recalled, when viewed in terms of the Messick and Jackson SDSVs, the "false" subscale of *ER-S* is keyed *against* the SD interpretation.

The correlations of the "false"-keyed portion of *ER-S* with Edwards' *SD* scale are, for the nine samples under consideration, .63, .61, .47, .73, .67, .50, .59, .56, and .38. These values again are at about the limits set by the respective reliabilities and support our earlier conclusion that the slight constant deviation between the absolute scale locations of the two sets of SDSVs is not empirically significant.

The relationship of the *ER-S* scale to the *Pt* scale must, of course, parallel the results obtained with the *SD* scale. For the nine samples, the correlations between *ER-S* and *Pt* were, respectively: —.80, —.75, —.67, —.79, —.79, —.67, —.66, —.70, and —.61. When due allowance is made for the attenuating effects of unreliability, these figures become, respectively: —1.00, —.95, —.93, —.95, —.97, —.85, —.93, —.94, and —.82. Again, the *ER-S* scale proves to be collinear with a scale which in turn is a marker variable for the Alpha dimension. But where previously the marker variables for the Alpha factor were susceptible to an interpretation in terms of SD, the *ER-S* scale as a new marker variable for the Alpha dimension may *not* be conceived in SD terms.

Because of the logic of its design, we may expect the *ER-S* scale to be a more subtle measure of the Alpha dimension than either the *SD* or *Pt* scale and therefore, less affected by deliberate attempts to fake good. One of the problems with the *SD* and *Pt* scales has been their tendency to produce highly skewed score distributions, when applied to reasonably normal, nonpsychiatric subject samples. For the *SD* scale, scores tend to cluster around a rather high mean and are skewed downward; for the *Pt* scale, scores usually cluster around a low mean and are skewed upwards. The *SD* and *Pt* normative data for Samples A through E, all samples without an obvious taint of psychopathology, are available in Table 18 and exemplify this frequent finding.

The interpretive dilemma presented by highly skewed score distributions in nonpsychopathological samples is that we cannot distinguish between scores genuinely betokening psychological health and equivalent scores which have been earned by an intelligent person seeking to simulate adjustment. None of the items in the SD scale create any uncertainty in a would-be simulator, because the criterion for item selection was precisely that there be no disagreement among simulating judges. The *Pt* scale, although not based upon the criterion of clarity for simulation, proves nevertheless to contain items which are almost totally unambiguous.

The *ER-S* scale, however, generates score distributions which are rarely far from symmetrical and, as a result, provides discriminations among subjects unseparated by such Alpha markers as

SD and *Pt*. The standard deviations developed by the *SD* and *Pt* scales vary widely and are especially small for the samples adjudged to be composed of healthy and generally intelligent individuals. The *ER-S* scale, on the other hand, develops appreciable standard deviations which fluctuate only slightly, and without any apparent order, over the nine samples. These psychometric properties, conjoined with (and doubtless a function of) the comparative contentual subtlety of the ER-S items suggest that this scale may not be so susceptible as earlier scales have been to the frequent and often entirely reasonable, tendency to fake good.

Finally, after mustering the various statistical supports of the *ER-S* scale, we may dare to look at the content of its items. Projection of a personality formulation from inspection of item content is not without its hazards, especially when the interpretation is not consensually or empirically validated. Nevertheless, we suggest that the ER-S items, though on balance uninfluenced by social desirability as objectified by scaling methods, portray an individual with a sense of personal identity and sufficiency. The high scorer on *ER-S* evidences an absence of undue, persistent introspection about self, body, and others; he is not crabby about the world around him and is neither cynical nor gushily credulous about its inhabitants. He is autonomous but not adamantly so; he has direction and stability rather than being diffuse and oscillating. The low scorer on the *ER-S* scale, on the other hand, is fitful, touchy, ruminative, and acutely aware of and bothered by himself as he participates in life. These are conjectures, limited in depth and completeness; the extent to which they are valid empirically may be ascertained in the next chapter.

8

BEHAVIORAL CORRELATES
OF THE FIRST TWO MMPI
FACTORS, ALPHA AND BETA

Almost none of the recent work proposing reinterpretation of the
MMPI in terms of acquiescence and of social desirability has
sought to support these alternative views by reference to behavioral data independent of the MMPI. Instead, most of the re-
interpreting arguments have been based upon the demonstration
of relationships between the MMPI and *a priori* or scaling-
constructed indices. However, where confounding continues to
exist, or is intrinsic to the measure being employed, the demonstration of such relationships cannot provide differential support
of competing interpretations. What is required is either unconfounding or resorting to fundamentally different domains of data
wherein certain interpretations are no longer supportable.

We have already, in earlier chapters, untied previously con-
nected interpretive dimensions and shown that, within the
MMPI, the response sets of acquiescence and social desirability
are not required for predicting MMPI responses. The analyses of
non-MMPI data now to be reported bring another and perhaps
more powerful basis for evaluation to bear on the problem of response sets, particularly in regard to the usefulness of the SD
concept. From such analyses can come the confluential recognitions which, when properly generalized back to situations where
the confounding is inescapable or argued for as convenient, deny
a previously irrepressible interpretation. In addition, in the pro-

tracted controversy which has surrounded the MMPI, there is something soul-satisfying in reality-testing the various interpretive contentions by concretely examining the behavior and personalities of individuals scoring high and scoring low on disputed dimensions. This method has proven powerful in the past (Block & Bailey, 1955; Gough, McKee, & Yandell, 1955) and was also used by Couch and Keniston. Unfortunately, in the last instance, as noted earlier, the acquiescence measure Couch and Keniston studied is open to significant criticism and so the behavioral correlates found by them may be variously interpreted.

In the present study, subjects in Samples A through E had been observed in various contexts by psychologists who recorded their assessments of each individual by means of a Q sort. These Q judgments, of course, were expressed in complete absence of knowledge as to the MMPI responses of the subjects. Thus, these data reflect the social-stimulus value or essential personalities of the subjects as they were observed and understood by the participating psychologists. The analyses to be reported were based upon a simple average or composite of all the Q sorts available for each subject. The context of observation, the Q set employed, and the number of observers differed in the various samples.

In Sample A, the subjects were observed over the course of a three-day intensive assessment and were judged by no less than six and usually eight psychologists. The Q set employed contained 76 items and was oriented toward behavioral description with some items requiring deeper level inferences.

In Sample B, the subjects were observed for 1½ hours during the course of which they interacted with their wives in several standardized social situations. Only one observer—a clinical psychologist—was present. The 72-item Q set used was oriented toward description of the interaction of the subject with his wife.

In Sample C, the subjects were interviewed for an average of 12 hours each. Each subject was Q sorted by his interviewer and by another psychologist who had read the verbatim record of the interview sessions. The Q deck employed was the 100-item California Q set (Block, 1961), which is oriented toward a psychodynamic personality description.

In Sample D, the subjects were Q sorted by an interviewing psychiatrist and by a psychologist who had administered the

Rorschach and TAT procedure. Two additional Q sorts were contributed by psychologists who formed an evaluation of the subject after studying the test protocols. The California Q set was employed.

In Sample E, the circumstances and procedures were as described for Sample C.

It is by no means suggested that these several procedures are of equal merit or optimal for the purposes of the present analysis. This kind of data is difficult to come by and considerations of availability have dictated their choice here.

Within each of the five samples, the Q sort composites of the Alpha Highs were contrasted, item by item, with the Q sort composites of the Alpha Lows using the *t* test to identify the discriminating Q variables. The results of these analyses are reported in Tables 19, 20, 21, 22, and 23. Parallel analyses of Beta Highs and Beta Lows were carried through to ascertain the behavioral significance of the Beta factor. The results are to be found in Tables 24, 25, 26, 27, and 28.

TABLE 19

Q Items Discriminating Alpha Highs from Alpha Lows, Sample A

ITEMS MORE CHARACTERISTIC OF ALPHA HIGHS (N = 20)

Significant at the .01 level
None

Significant at the .05 level
4. Emphasizes success and productive achievement as a means for achieving status, power and recognition.
18. Efficient, capable, able to mobilize resources easily and effectively; not bothered with work inhibitions.
22. Is verbally fluent; conversationally facile.
64. Tends to become ego-involved; makes personally relevant many different contexts.
67. Is persuasive; tends to win other people over to his point of view.
71. Communicates ideas clearly and effectively.

ITEMS MORE CHARACTERISTIC OF ALPHA LOWS (N = 20)

Significant at the .01 level
None

Significant at the .05 level
9. Has slow personal tempo; responds, speaks, and moves slowly.
51. Is cold and distant in his relationships with others.
74. Is unaware of his social stimulus value.

TABLE 20

Q Items Discriminating Alpha Highs from Alpha Lows, Sample B

ITEMS MORE CHARACTERISTIC OF ALPHA HIGHS ($N = 19$)

Significant at the .01 level
8. He expresses himself clearly.

Significant at the .05 level
6. He is proud of other.
29. He compliments other.
40. He trusts other.
42. He respects other.

ITEMS MORE CHARACTERISTIC OF ALPHA LOWS ($N = 20$)

Significant at the .01 level
None

Significant at the .05 level
15. He is demanding of other.
50. He is impatient with other.
51. He is stubborn.

TABLE 21

Q Items Discriminating Alpha Highs from Alpha Lows, Sample C

ITEMS MORE CHARACTERISTIC OF ALPHA HIGHS ($N = 17$)

Significant at the .01 level
75. Has a clear-cut, internally consistent personality. (*N.B. Amount* of information available before sorting is not intended here.)
84. Is cheerful. (*N.B.* Extreme placement toward uncharacteristic end of continuum implies gloominess.)

Significant at the .05 level
24. *Prides* self on being "objective," rational. (Regardless of whether person is really objective or rational.)
74. Is consciously unaware of self-concern; feels satisfied with self.

ITEMS MORE CHARACTERISTIC OF ALPHA LOWS ($N = 17$)

Significant at the .01 level
47. Tends to feel guilty. (*N.B.* Regardless of whether verbalized or not.)

Significant at the .05 level
10. Anxiety and tension find outlet in bodily symptoms. (*N.B.* If placed high, implies bodily dysfunction; if placed low, implies absence of autonomic arousal.)
82. Has fluctuating moods.

TABLE 22

Q Items Discriminating Alpha Highs from Alpha Lows, Sample D

ITEMS MORE CHARACTERISTIC OF ALPHA HIGHS ($N = 20$)

Significant at the .01 level

2. Is a genuinely dependable and responsible person.
3. Has a wide range of interests. (*N. B.* Superficiality or depth of interest is irrelevant here.)
8. Appears to have a high degree of intellectual capacity. (*N.B.* Whether actualized or not.) (*N.B.* Originality is not necessarily assumed.)
15. Is skilled in social techniques of imaginative play, pretending and humor.
17. Behaves in a sympathetic or considerate manner.
26. Is productive; gets things done.
28. Tends to arouse liking and acceptance in people.
29. Is turned to for advice and reassurance.
54. Emphasizes being with others; gregarious.
63. Judges self and others in conventional terms like "popularity," "the correct thing to do," social pressures, etc.
66. Enjoys aesthetic impressions; is aesthetically reactive.
71. Has high aspiration level for self.
84. Is cheerful. (*N.B.* Extreme placement toward uncharacteristic end of continuum implies unhappiness or depression.)
86. Handles anxiety and conflicts by, in effect, refusing to recognize their presence; repressive or dissociative tendencies.
88. Is personally charming.
92. Has social poise and presence; appears socially at ease.
93. Behaves in a feminine style and manner. (*N.B.* The cultural or subcultural conception is to be applied as a criterion.)

Significant at the .05 level

6. Is fastidious.
18. Initiates humor.
20. Has a rapid personal tempo; behaves and acts quickly.
24. Prides self on being "objective," rational.
35. Has warmth; has the capacity for close relationships; compassionate.
51. Genuinely values intellectual and cognitive matters. (*N.B.* Ability or achievement are not implied here.)
64. Is socially perceptive of a wide range of interpersonal cues.
98. Is verbally fluent; can express ideas well.

ITEMS MORE CHARACTERISTIC OF ALPHA LOWS ($N = 20$)

Significant at the .01 level

10. Anxiety and tension find outlet in bodily symptoms. (*N.B.* If placed high, implies bodily dysfunction; if placed low, implies absence of autonomic arousal.)

TABLE 22 (*Continued*)

22. Feels a lack of personal meaning in life.
30. Gives up and withdraws where possible in the face of frustration and adversity. (*N.B.* If placed high, implies generally defeatist; if placed low, implies counteractive.)
34. Over-reactive to minor frustrations; irritable.
38. Has hostility towards others. (*N.B.* Basic hostility is intended here; mode of expression is to be indicated by other items.)
39. Thinks and associates to ideas in unusual ways; has unconventional thought processes.
40. Is vulnerable to real or fancied threat, generally fearful.
45. Has a brittle ego-defense system; has a small reserve of integration; would be disorganized and maladaptive when under stress or trauma.
48. Keeps people at a distance; avoids close interpersonal relationships.
49. Is basically distrustful of people in general; questions their motivations.
55. Is self-defeating.
59. Is concerned with own body and the adequacy of its physiological functioning.
78. Feels cheated and victimized by life; self-pitying.
79. Tends to ruminate and have persistent, preoccupying thoughts.
82. Has fluctuating moods.
85. Emphasizes communication through action and non-verbal behavior.

Significant at the .05 level

16. Is introspective and concerned with self as an object. (*N.B.* Introspectiveness per se does not imply insight.)
46. Engages in personal fantasy and daydreams, fictional speculations.
50. Is unpredictable and changeable in behavior and attitudes.
62. Tends to be rebellious and non-conforming.
65. Characteristically pushes and tries to stretch limits; sees what he can get away with.
100. Does not vary roles; relates to everyone in the same way.

TABLE 23

Q Items Discriminating Alpha Highs from Alpha Lows, Sample E

Items More Characteristic of Alpha Highs ($N = 18$)

Significant at the .01 level

15. The "light touch" as compared to the "heavy touch."
33. Is calm, relaxed in manner.
54. Emphasizes being with others; gregarious.
74. Is consciously unaware of self-concern; feels satisfied with self.
84. Is cheerful. (*N.B.* Extreme placement toward uncharacteristic end of continuum implies gloominess.)
92. Has social poise and presence; appears socially at ease.

TABLE 23 *(Continued)*

Significant at the .05 level

3. Has a wide range of interests. (*N.B.* Superficiality or depth of interest is irrelevant here.)
18. Initiates humor.
26. Is productive; gets things done. (Regardless of speed.)
28. Tends to arouse liking and acceptance in people.
29. Is turned to for advice and reassurance.
31. Is satisfied with physical appearance.
56. Responds to humor.
63. Judges self and others in conventional terms like "popularity," "the correct thing to do," social pressures, etc.
95. Tends to proffer advice.

ITEMS MORE CHARACTERISTIC OF ALPHA LOWS ($N = 13$)

Significant at the .01 level

22. Feels a lack of personal meaning in life. (Uncharacteristic end means zest.)
40. Is vulnerable to real or fancied threat, generally fearful.
68. Is basically anxious.
72. Over-concerned with own adequacy as a person, either at conscious or unconscious levels. (*N.B.* A clinical judgment is required here; number 74 reflects subjective satisfaction with self.)

Significant at the .05 level

39. Thinks and associates to ideas in unusual ways; has unconventional thought processes. (Either pathological or creative.)
47. Tends to feel guilty. (*N.B.* Regardless of whether verbalized or not.)
48. Aloof, keeps people at a distance; avoids close interpersonal relationships.
78. Feels cheated and victimized by life.
79. Tends to ruminate and have persistent, preoccupying thoughts (Either pathological or creative).
82. Has fluctuating moods.
87. Interprets basically simple and clear-cut situations in complicated and particularizing ways.
89. Compares self to others. Is alert to real or fancied differences between self and other people.

TABLE 24

Q Items Discriminating Beta Highs from Beta Lows, Sample A

ITEMS MORE CHARACTERISTIC OF BETA HIGHS ($N = 20$)

Significant at the .01 level

9. Has slow personal tempo; responds, speaks and moves slowly.

TABLE 24 *(Continued)*

11. Is a conscientious, responsible, dependable person.
21. Is stereotyped and unoriginal in his approach to problems.
24. With respect to authority, is submissive, compliant and overly accepting.
28. Tends to side-step troublesome situations; makes concessions to avoid unpleasantness.
34. Conforming; tends to do the things that are prescribed.
35. Respects others; is permissive and accepting; not judgmental.
42. Is unable to make decisions without vacillation, hesitation or delay.
50. Over-controls his impulses; is inhibited; needlessly delays or denies gratification.

Significant at the .05 level

1. Derives personal reward and pleasure from his work; values productive achievement for its own sake.
7. Has a narrow range of interests.
8. Gets along well in the world as it is; is socially appropriate in his behavior; keeps out of trouble. (*N.B.* To be considered as conceptually separate from the subject's internal psychic state.)
17. Is rigid; inflexible in thought and action.
20. Lacks social poise and presence; becomes rattled and upset in social situations.
25. Is a likeable person. (*N.B.* The subject's general acceptability rather than the rater's personal reactions is intended.)
31. Lacks confidence in his own ability.
41. Is natural; free from pretense; unaffected.
47. Is self-abasing; feels unworthy, guilty, humble, given to self-blame.
56. Is pedantic and fussy about minor things.
74. Is unaware of his social stimulus value.

ITEMS MORE CHARACTERISTIC OF BETA LOWS ($N = 20$)

Significant at the .01 level

4. Emphasizes success and productive achievement as a means for achieving status, power and recognition.
6. Is guileful and potentially deceitful.
12. Manipulates people as a means to achieving personal ends; opportunistic; sloughs over the meaning and value of the individual.
14. Is competitive with his peers; likes to be ahead and win.
15. Takes an ascendant role in his relations with others.
33. Tends to arouse hostility and resentment in other people.
45. Under-controls his impulses; acts with insufficient thinking and deliberation; unable to delay gratifications.
61. Is aggressive and hostile in his personal relations.
64. Tends to become ego-involved; makes personally relevant many different contexts.

TABLE 24 (*Continued*)

65. Is sarcastic and cynical.
66. Emphasizes oral pleasure; self-indulgent.
72. Is rebellious toward authority figures, rules and other constraints.
73. Tends to be ostentatious and exhibitionistic.
76. Is an expressive, ebullient person; colorful.

Significant at the .05 level

2. Has a high degree of intellectual ability.
22. Is verbally fluent; conversationally facile.
48. Is self-defensive; rationalizes, excuses, blames.
52. Seeks and enjoys aesthetic and sensuous impressions.
60. Takes the initiative in social relations.
67. Is persuasive; tends to win other people over to his point of view.
71. Communicates ideas clearly and effectively.

TABLE 25

Q Items Discriminating Beta Highs from Beta Lows, Sample **B**

ITEMS MORE CHARACTERISTIC OF BETA HIGHS ($N = 20$)

Significant at the .01 level

7. He opposes other indirectly, without openly disagreeing or being frank.
19. He is deceiving and subtle in his manipulations of other.
66. He confuses other.

Significant at the .05 level

17. He hides his feelings from other.
35. He keeps other at a distance.
52. He belittles himself with other.
54. He apologizes for himself.
58. He is inhibited in this situation.

ITEMS MORE CHARACTERISTIC OF BETA LOWS ($N = 21$)

Significant at the .01 level

9. When he disagrees, he tries to talk it over with other.
27. He is straightforward and frank with other.
31. He understands other as a person.

Significant at the .05 level

8. He expresses himself clearly.
24. He gives other help.
42. He respects other.
62. He is emotionally responsive to other.
70. He has a sense of humor.

TABLE 26

Q Items Discriminating Beta Highs from Beta Lows, Sample C

ITEMS MORE CHARACTERISTIC OF BETA HIGHS ($N = 17$)

Significant at the .01 level

2. Is a genuinely dependable and responsible person.
6. Is fastidious.
7. Favors conservative values in a variety of areas.
17. Behaves in a sympathetic or considerate manner.
25. Tends toward over-control of needs and impulses; binds tensions excessively; delays gratification unnecessarily.
26. Is productive; gets things done. (Regardless of speed.)
33. Is calm, relaxed in manner.
70. *Behaves* in an ethically consistent manner; is consistent with own personal standards.

Significant at the .05 level

5. Behaves in a giving way toward others. (*N.B.* Regardless of the motivation involved.)
16. Is introspective. (*N.B.* Introspectiveness per se does not imply insight.)
41. Is moralistic. (*N.B.* Regardless of the particular nature of the moral code.)
71. Has high aspiration level for self.
75. Has a clear-cut, internally consistent personality. (*N.B. Amount* of information available before sorting is not intended here.)
92. Has social poise and presence; appears socially at ease.
97. Is emotionally bland; has flattened affect.
100. Does not vary roles; relates to everyone in the same way.

ITEMS MORE CHARACTERISTIC OF BETA LOWS ($N = 17$)

Significant at the .01 level

43. Is facially and/or gesturally expressive.
50. Is unpredictable and changeable in behavior and attitudes.
52. *Behaves* in an assertive fashion in interpersonal situations. (*N.B.* Item 14 reflects underlying submissiveness; this refers to overt behavior.)
53. Tends toward under-control of needs and impulses; unable to delay gratification.
62. Tends to be rebellious and non-conforming.
65. Characteristically pushes and tries to stretch limits; see what he can get away with.
67. Is self-indulgent.
73. Tends to perceive many different contexts in sexual terms; eroticizes situations.
82. Has fluctuating moods.

TABLE 26 *(Continued)*

94. Expresses hostile feelings directly.
99. Is self-dramatizing; histrionic.

Significant at the .05 level

 4. Is a talkative individual.
34. Over-reactive to minor frustrations; irritable.
45. Has a brittle ego-defense system; has a small reserve of integration; would be disorganized and maladaptive when under stress or trauma.
49. Is basically distrustful of people in general; questions their motivations.
58. Enjoys sensuous experiences (including touch, taste, smell, physical contact).
76. Tends to project his own feelings and motivations onto others.

TABLE 27

Q Items Discriminating Beta Highs from Beta Lows, Sample D

ITEMS MORE CHARACTERISTIC OF BETA HIGHS (*N = 20*)

Significant at the .01 level

 7. Favors conservative values in a variety of areas.
 9. Is uncomfortable with uncertainty and complexities.
40. Is vulnerable to real or fancied threat, generally fearful.
42. Reluctant to commit self to any definite course of action; tends to delay or avoid action.
70. Behaves in an ethically consistant manner; is consistent with own personal standards.
100. Does not vary roles; relates to everyone in the same way.

Significant at the .05 level

14. Genuinely submissive; accepts domination comfortably.
25. Tends toward over-control of needs and impulses; binds tensions excessively; delays gratification unnecessarily.
30. Gives up and withdraws where possible in the face of frustration and adversity. (*N.B.* If placed high, implies generally defeatist; if placed low, implies counteractive.)
48. Keeps people at a distance; avoids close interpersonal relationships.
75. Has a clear-cut, internally consistent personality. (*N.B.* Amount of information available before sorting is not intended here.)
97. Is emotionally bland; has flattened affect.

ITEMS MORE CHARACTERISTIC OF BETA LOWS (*N = 20*)

Significant at the .01 level

 3. Has a wide range of interests (*N.B.* Superficiality or depth of interest is irrelevant here.)

TABLE 27 *(Continued)*

4. Is a talkative individual.
8. Appears to have a high degree of intellectual capacity. (*N.B.* Whether actualized or not.) (*N.B.* Originality is not necessarily assumed.)
37. Is guileful and deceitful, manipulative, opportunistic.
98. Is verbally fluent; can express ideas well.

Significant at the .05 level

10. Anxiety and tension find outlet in bodily symptoms. (*N.B.* If placed high, implies bodily dysfunction; if placed low, implies absence of autonomic arousal.)
23. Extrapunitive; tends to transfer or project blame.
51. Genuinely values intellectual and cognitive matters. (*N.B.* Ability or achievement is not implied here.)
53. Various needs tend toward relatively direct and uncontrolled expression; unable to delay gratification.
59. Is concerned with own body and the adequacy of its physiological functioning.
62. Tends to be rebellious and non-conforming.
82. Has fluctuating moods.

TABLE 28

Q Items Discriminating Beta Highs from Beta Lows, Sample E

Items More Characteristic of Beta Highs (*N* = 16)

Significant at the .01 level

70. Behaves in an ethically consistent manner; is consistent with own personal standards.

Significant at the .05 level

2. Is a genuinely dependable and responsible person.
7. Favors conservative values in a variety of areas.
41. Is moralistic. (*N.B.* Regardless of the particular nature of the moral code.)
47. Tends to feel guilty. (*N.B.* Regardless of whether verbalized or not.)
75. Has a clear-cut, internally consistent personality. (*N.B. Amount* of information available before sorting is not intended here.)

Items More Characteristic of Beta Lows (*N* = 17)

Significant at the .01 level

92. Has social poise and presence; appears socially at ease.

Significant at the .05 level

4. Is a talkative individual.
46. Engages in personal fantasy and daydreams, fictional speculations.
56. Responds to humor.

TABLE 28 *(Continued)*

67. Is self-indulgent.
73. Tends to perceive many different contexts in sexual terms; eroticizes situations.
88. Is personally charming.
99. Is self-dramatizing; histrionic.

These tables require some comment. It should be noted that the number of Q items reaching the .05 level of significance varies widely from sample to sample. It is impossible (and unnecessary) to separate out the several reasons for this fluctuation. Certainly contributing are the differential reliabilities of the Q judgments as a function of the number of sorters involved and the scope of their observations (at least six judges observing over a three-day period contributed to the Q formulations of Sample A; one judge observing subjects for 90 minutes contributed to Q sorts analyzed for Sample B); the different degrees of extremeness of the comparisons being made (in Sample A, two groups of 20 were selected from a total pool of 100; in Sample E, groups of 16 and 17 were selected from a total pool of 49); and intrinsically different characteristics of the subject samples.

If we consider the *number* of statistically discriminating Q items as indicative of the behavioral potency of the MMPI factor involved, then in the three samples composed of males (Samples A, B, and C), the Beta dimension appears to have more consequence than the Alpha factor. For the two samples consisting of women (Samples D and E), the Alpha dimension has more behavioral ramifications than the Beta factor. Looking over the results from all five samples, it is clear that in nonpsychiatric samples, the Beta dimension is at least as behaviorally decisive as the Alpha factor, although the Alpha dimension is much more heavily emphasized within the MMPI. Doubtless, in samples containing individuals with a wider range of psychopathology—samples more appropriate to the initial intent and aspiration of the MMPI—the Alpha factor would enjoy the larger number of behavioral correlates. Overall, however, both MMPI factors possess independent behavioral correlates which are numerous, coherent, and of indisputable importance.

Naming the First Factor of the MMPI

Looking first at the results surrounding Alpha, it is apparent from Tables 19 through 23 that Alpha Highs are individuals perceived by psychologists as being genuinely psychologically healthy—they are evaluated as integrated and yet open to experience, able to cope resourcefully with their complex worlds. Alpha Highs are not feigning adjustment, as the SD formulation would require.

Alpha Lows, on the other hand, are in fact more disturbed and more brittle individuals—they are relatively vulnerable before life's inevitable stresses and, as a result, have chosen to participate less fully in their experience. Alpha Lows are not fairly construed simply as individuals in whom the tendency to emit socially desirable responses is reduced. It appears from these analyses that more than facade or an absence of facade was involved in the manner in which these several sets of subjects responded to the MMPI. In significant ways, these individuals conveyed some truths about themselves to which an interpretation in terms of SD does an injustice since the term, "social desirability," inevitably connotes pretense at some level. The present data indicate pretension cannot be assumed. On the other hand, the behavioral hypotheses which issue from a characterological view of Alpha as related to, say, differences along an adaptability-vulnerability personality dimension are well supported.

If the first MMPI factor is not to be understood profitably in terms of the SD concept, just how should this dimension be construed in the light of the current analyses? Welsh's (1956) earlier identification of this factor as "anxiety" would appear to be improved if changed to "susceptibility to anxiety." Anxiety is a *state* of the individual where this factor reflects a *characterological disposition*. In other factor analyses of the MMPI, this repeatedly found first component has been variously identified as, for example, "psychoticism" (Wheeler, *et al.*, 1951) or "general maladjustment" (Tyler, 1951) and when reversed as "social appropriateness" (Block & Bailey, 1955) or "ego-strength" (Kassebaum, Couch, & Slater, 1959). None of these labels seems conceptually satisfactory when referenced to the behavioral correlates of this factor, as reported here. Psychotics may well place low on the Alpha dimension but other, clearly nonpsychotic individuals also will be Alpha Lows. "General maladjustment" and "social appropriateness" perhaps are not incorrect as descriptive labels but they are labels with no conceptual properties, no position within a theoretical framework from which predictions will flow. The term, "ego-strength," is by now conceptually amorphous and used diversely, often simply as a jargonistic substitute for "adjustment."

The reader has before him the data from which he can form his own understanding of the first MMPI factor. However, the writer cannot forego the opportunity of indicating his own current conception of the significance of this MMPI dimension.

It is suggested that this factor be identified as "ego-resiliency." The word, resilient, implies the resourcefulness, adaptability, and engagement with his world that characterizes the individual placed high on this continuum; the word, ego, implies that an enduring, structural aspect of personality is involved. In conjunction, the term ego-resiliency, is intended to denote the individual's characteristic adaptation capability when under the strain set by new environmental demands. Alpha Highs appear to react to the press of new and yet unmastered circumstances in resourceful, tenacious, but elastic ways and so may be termed ego-resilient. Alpha Lows, on the other hand, have small adaptive margins and consequently react to their stresses in rigidified or chaotic ways. Because they are not ego-resilient, they are unable to respond effectively to the dynamic requirements of their situation.

An individual who is unresilient will not be in a *state* of anxiety if the circumstances in which he functions are for him safe and predictable. Yet, it may be expected that, inevitably, an adaptively inelastic individual will find a wider range of environmental happenings to be disruptive of his personal economy, and distressing. Accordingly, he will present himself as more anxious, more maladjusted, less appropriate, less attuned to this world and, not least, as possessing personal attributes which society agrees are undesirable.

Thus, the concept of ego-resiliency fits well the behavioral correlates of the first MMPI factor and can encompass the various interpretations previously offered of this dimension. The construct has the further advantages, moreover, of fitting into a theoretical framework, of not being tied to a particular evaluative society or culture as a referent, and of predicting to additional and diverse environmental contexts; *e.g.*, ego-resilient individuals, as measured by the MMPI, should be able to track a dynamic stimulus more accurately than individuals who are inelastic; ego-resiliency, as measured by the MMPI, should relate—when relevant other variables are held constant—to both the ability to resist distractions and the ability to associate in distant, even bizarre ways when instructed to do so ("regression in the service of the ego"). For the several reasons, it is suggested that the first factor within the MMPI be identified as the Ego-Resiliency (ER) dimension.

For the present, the Alpha or Ego-Resiliency factor of the MMPI may be measured reasonably effectively by such established MMPI scales—scored in appropriate directions—as *SD*, *Pt*, *Pn*, and *A*. In the same tradition but with superior reliability is the Ego-Resiliency (Obvious) (*ER-O*) scale, listed and described in Appendix A. The *ER-O* scale consists of 108 items, "true" and "false" balanced, all related at the .01 level of significance to the Alpha dimension but not selected with any reference to SD scale values.

All of these scales are susceptible to deliberate feigning attempts or to tendencies to deny—for reasons of which the responding individual may be unaware—actually existing personal frailities. Where the possibility of deliberate deception or personally unacknowledged defensiveness exists—that is, high *L* or *K* scores—the previously described *ER-S* scale is likely to be useful because of its content-subtlety and control for social desirability. Credence should be given to an individual's placement on the first factor of the MMPI only when it seems safe to presume that the tendency to "fake good" did not significantly effect his responses.

NAMING THE SECOND FACTOR OF THE MMPI

Considering now the nature of the Beta-discriminating Q items (Tables 24 through 28), it may be seen that earlier clinical understandings of this MMPI component as related to the containment or expression of impulse are both solidified and extended. As we read the Beta analyses—and the reader has available before him the information on which he may base his own conclusions—in all five samples, in diverse yet coherent ways, the Beta Highs and Beta Lows appear to differ in the extent to which they suppress impulse or are spontaneous with it. There seem to be differences between the sexes in the way impulse is modulated, but that a dimension akin to impulse-control underlies these several comparisons does not appear in doubt. The results involving Sample B—although sparse perhaps because of the brevity of the observations and because only one observer was involved—are especially interesting in that they indicate the interpersonal consequences of different modes of impulse expression.

Earlier, Welsh (1956) labeled a similar MMPI dimension as "repression," a title that in view of the present analyses now seems over-extended and only partially adequate. The notion of repression carries implications going well beyond simple impulse suppression, implications for which the current findings offer none of the special support required. To validate an interpretation in terms of repression necessitates demonstration of a specific sequence of intrapsychic events culminating in a discrepancy between awareness and intention on the one hand and behavior and expression on the other. Precisely because the concept of repression is complex, it requires special contrapositions of data for its support, and the personological correlates of the Beta dimension simply are insufficient for this task.

Kassebaum, Couch, and Slater (1959), having achieved the usual factor structure of the MMPI, interpret the Beta dimension in terms of "introversion-extroversion." They acknowledge the unusualness of this interpretation but are motivated to link their results to Eysenck's views on the dimensionality of human personality (1953). Their reasoning stems primarily from the labels of the MMPI scales they analyzed and not further behavioral data.

Welsh's *R* scale, possessor of the highest loading on the Beta factor in the Kassebaum, Couch, and Slater analysis, is reinterpreted by these authors as a measure of cautiousness and inhibition, and hence of introversion. The introversion construction is considered further affirmed by the positive loadings earned by the *D* and *Social Introversion* scales and, less clearly, by scales labeled *Achievement via Conformance* and *Originality Potential*. As conceptual support for these loadings, Kassebaum, Couch, and Slater cite Eysenck citing Guilford and Guilford who say:

> It would seem that there is some basis for lumping together some characteristics bordering on seclusiveness with some implying a thinking person and still others that indicate depressed emotional tendencies and calling the resultant the introvert (Kassebaum, Couch, & Slater, 1959, p. 229; Eysenck, 1953, p. 104; Guilford & Guilford, 1939, p. 34).

The extravert is viewed by Kassebaum, Couch, and Slater as one who is "expressive and labile, and cathects new activities easily" (p. 230) and who shows "id predominance over superego activities" (p. 229). They also related the "yea-saying" tendency, as studied by Couch and Keniston (1961), to extraversion.

Conceptual preferences are in no small part esthetic preferences and in these latter terms, this writer finds the conceptualization of Kassebaum, Couch, and Slater, of Eysenck, and of Guilford and Guilford, to be unsatisfying. Concepts should be integrates, not amalgams, and "lumping together" is hardly the way to achieve variables of unequivocal dimensionality. In particular, the formulation of introversion-extroversion advanced by Eysenck and accepted by Kassebaum, Couch, and Slater couples and confuses the dimensions of "constriction-expression" and "inward turning-outward turning" when both theoretically and empirically, as our Beta correlates show, these dimensions are separable. Impulsivity does not preclude the concomitant tendency for introspectiveness; constriction does not necessarily entail a rich inner life. If a distinction between impulse regulation and inner-outer orientation is held to be useful, as argued here, then it would be perhaps most faithful to the original and connotative meaning of the terms, introversion-extraversion, to restrict their definition to the focusing of attention on inner stimuli or on outer stimuli. In so doing, identification of the Beta dimension of the MMPI as introversion-extraversion no longer is tenable because this factor centrally relates to impulse monitoring per se.

Our own predilection—it may not be surprising—together with a desire for concepts that are not method-bound is to view the present behavioral results as arguing well for an interpretation in terms of over- and under-control as earlier formulated and experimentally studied (*cf.*, Block, J., 1950; Block, Jeanne H., 1951; Block & Block, 1951; Block & Block, 1952; Block & Thomas, 1955; Block & Martin, 1955).

The construct of ego-control relates to the individual's characteristic mode of monitoring impulse. When dimensionalized, the underlying continuum is conceived as representing excessive containment of impulse and delay of gratification at the one end (over-control) versus insufficient modulation of impulse and an inability to delay gratification at the other end (under-control). Behaviorally, an over-controller appears to be constrained and distant, with minimal expression of his personal emotions; he is highly organized and categorical in his thinking, tending to adhere rigidly to previous understandings; he can continue to work on uninteresting tasks for long periods of time; he is over-conforming, indecisive, and with narrow and relatively unchanging interests; he delays gratification even when pleasure is a sensible course of action, not threatening of long range intents.

Behaviorally, an under-controller is unduly spontaneous, with enthusiasms neither held in check nor long sustained; his decisions are made (and unmade) rapidly and his emotional fluctuations are readily visible; he disregards, if he does not disdain, social customs and mores; he tends toward immediate gratification of his desires even when such gratification is inconsistent with the reality of his situation or his own ultimate goals; his grooves for behavior are not deeply ingrained and, accordingly, his actions can frequently cut across conventional categories of response in ways that are (for better or for worse) original (Block & Turula, 1963).

Because the construct of ego-control fits the present data well and no clearly better conceptual alternative looms on the scene, we suggest that the second factor within the MMPI be identified as the Ego-Control (EC) dimension.

For the moment, reasonably adequate MMPI scales to measure the Beta or second dimension are the *EC-3, EC-4* and *R* scales. The *EC-5* scale, a fifth version of an MMPI scale to measure this component, is described in Appendix B and may be preferable because of its generally higher reliability and because it is "true" and "false" balanced. But all of these scales are less than what is realizable because they all fail to respect some important differences between the sexes in the way over- and under-control is expressed.

Although there has been a general, and understandable, reluctance among scale constructors to employ different scales for men and for women, here is one instance, we believe, where a substantial improvement in the measurement of a dimension may result if separate scale construction is applied. With respect to ego-control, the culture tends to encourage or at least sanction impulsivity in the male while discouraging such behavior in the female. Thus, consider the items: "38. During one period when I was a youngster I engaged in petty thievery; 471. In school my marks in deportment were quite regularly bad." A response of "true" to these items is related to under-control in males but not in females.

As a further source of valid variance lost when sex differences are not respected, there are items which have one significance when responded to by males but rather different meanings in a feminine context. Thus, a response of "true" to the item, "441. I like tall women," is an indicator of under-control in men but is not a discriminator among women. A response of "true" to the item, "435. Usually I prefer to work with women," is scored for over-control in women but does not distinguish among men.

Because of cultural conditioning and the interaction of sex category with ego-control, separate *EC* scales for men and for women would appear to be desirable. Preliminary versions of such scales, labled *EC-5M* and *EC-5W* are to be found in Appendix B, together with some of their descriptive statistics. Further work is continuing on developing sex-specific ego-control scales but not within the MMPI-item pool.

9

IMPLICATIONS FOR RESEARCH
ON STRUCTURED
PERSONALITY INVENTORIES

The weary reader, if he has been persuaded by the data and arguments brought forward in the preceding chapters, may well wonder whether the acquiescence and social desirability challenges to the MMPI and the responses engendered by these reinterpretations have resulted in any net advance in the understanding of structured personality inventories. In these concluding remarks, and in a more frankly personal way, I would like to indicate some of the conclusions impressed upon me in the course of these obsessive analysis.

It will be helpful if in the future there develops a closer, reciprocal communication between the clinical users of inventories and the statistical analysts of these procedures. In retrospect, it seems clear that some unfortunate or unnecessary analytical and interpretive excursions might have been avoided if the appreciable knowledge and lore surrounding the MMPI, only part of which is in the literature, had been known to investigators about to begin a correlational study. Not all clinically derived lore is valid and certainly such beliefs may not be accepted on faith. But neither is clinical experience entirely solipsistic and therefore automatically to be neglected. If the clinical solution is not always, or satisfactorily a "context of justification" (Reichenbach, 1950), it is always and perhaps the necessary "context of discovery." There is a voluminous amount of literature surrounding the clinical usage and results developed by the MMPI (*cf.*, Hathaway & Meehl, 1951; Dahlstrom & Welsh, 1960) and awareness of this background prior to statistical analysis would have added needed perspective to many of the studies which have appeared. Findings generating the "aha" phenomenon in some investigators arouse only an "of course" reaction in other psychologists when there has been inadequate communication.

A second observation has been that downright carelessness has sometimes characterized ambitiously interpreted studies. By and large, correlational analysis of inventory scales is a simple endeavor these days. Computers are abundantly available and it is easy enough to score a bunch of MMPI protocols, to correlate these scores, and then to factor-analyze.

However, ease of analysis should not mean casualness in regard to the scales chosen for study. On occasion, scales have been employed in circumstances which can only mean ignorance or naïvete. These are harsh words but consider the following: several correlational studies in the response set domain have employed both the Prejudice (*Pr*) and Tolerance (*To*) scales of the MMPI. Both of these scales are due to Gough (1951; 1952). The *Pr* scale was developed and validated as an MMPI measure to correlate with the California Ethnocentrism-Fascism Scale (Adorno *et al.*, 1950). Later, Gough decided to revise the *Pr* scale slightly and for entirely appropriate conceptual reasons took the occasion to relabel the scale as a measure of tolerance, reversing the direction of scoring of the items. In the *To* scale, 29 of the 30 items overlap with the *Pr* scale but scored oppositely.

Since the sample of scales selected for study can determine the shape of the results obtained, simple considerations of availability must be bolstered by actual knowledge of candidate scales. To use *both* the *Pr* and the *To* scales in the same study and draw weighty conclusions from their opposite but identical factor loadings is informative only about the investigators. A related problem here has been the tendency to employ scales widely differing with regard to the quality of their validation and to use scales which, in the aggregate, overemphasize one aspect of the MMPI while underrepresenting another. Again, there are indications that primary sources of knowledge about the scales to be evaluated were not consulted because differential evaluation has not been accorded scales of differential quality; impressive relationships have not been recognized as due to redundant scale selection.

A third quality of research on response sets has been the "belle indifference" or bland imperturbability displayed in the face of newly uncovered relationships arguing against the revisionist approach. Thus, a finding that imprisoned subjects earn their peak and rather high MMPI score on the *Pd* scale is noted but somehow does not affect an ultimate interpretation of the dimension underlying *Pd* in terms of acquiescence. Repeated findings that hospitalized psychiatric patients score higher on the clinical scales of the MMPI have been assimilated to an acquiescence or SD explanation. The interpretive rule appears to have been to value relationships existing among MMPI scales and indices more highly than relationships existing between the MMPI and external behavioral criteria. As we have seen, exclusive reliance on procedure-bound measures or analyses offers no protection against fortuitous or otherwise unrecognized linkages that are conceptually misleading.

I believe the analyses reported in this monograph support rather well the MMPI as initially conceived and as traditionally employed. Preliminary analysis of the California Psychological Inventory (CPI), by the methods described earlier, suggests that it too can deny interpretation in terms of acquiescence (Jackson, 1960) and social desirability. My own conjecture is that response-set interpretations of still other inventories administered in personally involving circumstances will, under close scrutiny, also prove inadequate. Although for many inventory users, there will be only confirmation of expectations within these pages, the usefulness of our sequence of analyses has been to confront the response-set position on its own terms and to show how these interpretations—although now proven insufficient—happened to be awarded the possibility of truth. At the same time, some of the analyses extend our understanding of the behaviors indexed by the MMPI and suggest some directions of constructive change that are necessary if we are to improve our methods for personality assessment. The MMPI is now a quarter of a century old, and it is not surprising if some deficiencies in it have become apparent or the potentialities of later thinking are not realized within its framework. Given the hard-won indications of the fruitfulness of the MMPI approach, it may now be the time to take another big leap forward, toward the next generation of personality inventories.

Four kinds of change to improve the MMPI and related structured personality inventories may be indicated, and will be remarked upon briefly. These are: (1) the use of broader item pools; (2) the use of more sophisticated and more conceptual models for scale development; (3) the use of more intensive and extensive empirical analyses; and (4) the strengthening of the criteria for scale validation.

BROADENING ITEM POOLS

As we have seen, the MMPI-item pool heavily weights a first factor relating essentially to adjustment. For an inventory oriented toward psychiatric diagnosis, this emphasis is perhaps desirable but the redundancy does seem inordinate. Further, when it is recognized that the MMPI has come to be applied as a broadguage personality inventory in nonpsychiatric settings, then a good many of its items appear to be irrelevant (and affronting) in this larger context. The CPI, although emphasizing this first factor less, still contains about 200 of the MMPI items and does not represent a truly radical break with the MMPI-item pool, for it appears to have roughly the same factor structure as the MMPI (Mitchell & Pierce-Jones, 1960; Nichols & Schnell, 1963).

In the light of past experience in using the MMPI, it would appear desirable to evolve an item pool which diminishes the pervasiveness of the first MMPI factor. At the same time, the items sufficiently representing this necessary dimension should be so constructed as to camouflage their pertinence to social criteria. The problem of faking exists primarily with regard to the first factor and a stronger version of a scale like the ER-S measure could be the way to index this dimension in nonobvious ways. Unfortunately, the currently available version of the ER-S scale, although possessing a conventional enough reliability, cannot be improved appreciably because of the absence of further or better items meeting the criteria of social neutrality but Alpha-relevance.

The use of socially neutral items can be expected to encourage a more congenial reception of an inventory among relatively normal subjects. In the MMPI, there are a good many impertinent items precipitating vehement rejection by nonpsychotic subjects. Such subjects often react against the inventory procedure because of the inanity, for them, of many of the items to which they must respond. In modifying or developing items to achieve a more general applicability, there would appear to be no reason in principle why the resulting inventory should be less effective in diagnosing the extremes and kinds of psychopathology. As a positive by-product of this approach, we may anticipate improved discriminations among nonpsychiatric subjects on new or extended personality dimensions.

In improving or assembling an item pool, there should be greater recognition of the ways in which implicit theoretical conceptions or implicit value systems may affect item writing or selection. Thus, in the MMPI, it seems to me there are very few statements relating to the dimensions of introspectiveness and the few such items to be found all taint inner life with neuroticism or worse, *e.g.*, "349. I have strange and peculiar thoughts."

As a further impression, I am struck by the extent to which the MMPI discourages the admission of spontaneity and nonconformity as a way of adjustment and "pulls" instead for a Puritan ethic, self-control almost to the point of constriction, and a "don't rock the boat" approach to life. The problem posed by implicit theoretical and value preconceptions is always with us, but acknowledgment of its presence and sensitivity to the operation of these influences can prevent foreclosed findings which verify only the status quo.

Finally, under this heading, I note the great need and potential of inventory items tapping salient personality variables now inadequately reflected or touching upon personality constructs not yet encompassed by the inventory approach. The dimensional possibilities are rich and of course take various forms according to the special theory being promulgated. Here I wish only to observe that, with the exception of Cattell's efforts (Cattell & Stice, 1962), there appears to be no grand attempt to create new inventory terrain. Most inventory-item pools are, when not highly derivative, impressively equivalent in the kind of items included, differing only in the relative emphasis of the few components considered. Yet, I am convinced many more and highly significant areas of human experience and functioning may be manifested through structured personality inventories than is presently the case. We should try to gain these additional personality indicators by broadening the coverage attained by an item pool.

Using More Sophisticated Models for Scale Development

The empirical approach to scale construction has been to identify items responded to differentially by criterion groups, defining these items as a scale. For most scale constructors (and I include my usual self), the problem of the model underlying the scale does not explicitly arise. In these circumstances, the "single common factor" model for scales is not an inappropriate one. Indeed, it is a good basis from which to start since it is wise to see just how far a simple model can take us before jettisoning it and assuming the burden of more complicated models.

The logical and practical deficiency of inventory scales, however, is that a given score may be variously earned and therefore may have varying significance. In part, this weakness of scales can be remedied by greater attention to such orthodox psychometric properties as internal consistency and discrimination capacity. Many empirical scales are far from achieving the psychometric quality that might be reached with further care. However, a bound exists on scale improvements simply from greater attention and refinement when the underlying psychological construct is behaviorally complex in its manifestations.

Thus, the psychodynamically important notions of "alternative manifestations" or "the similarity of opposites"—of behaviors related disjunctively instead of additively—wreaks havoc with the "single common factor" model of inventory scales as usually conceived since the intercorrelations of items expressing alternative manifestations of a given variable will be negative. If heuristically guided by psychological theory, however, psychometric analyses may identify functionally interchangeable but reciprocally related items and rescue them for the "single common factor" model by redefining their conjunction as a single, but derived, "item."

A more complicated way of conceptualizing the psychometric relations underlying the total score earned on a scale is in terms of what may be called the "cancellation" or "variance suppression" model. In this model, the response to a particular item may have equivocal import—it identifies the subset of subjects for whom the scale dimension or category *may* be relevant excluding those subjects who clearly do not belong. Other items are then required to further partition this first subset. Some of these other items may bring to bear additional signs or indicators of the focal construct. But, still other items may operate to identify (and hence screen out) foreign or irrelevant personality predispositions that thus far have proceeded down the common-response path. Besides selecting the correct individuals by employing diversified signs as a basis for diagnosis, it is also useful to eliminate wrongly categorized subjects by noting the responses to items identifying antithetical constructs. Antithetical items will not relate positively to the scale dimension but will correlate with certain items in the scale. They operate to cancel the irrelevant variance in another item, enhancing as a consequence that item's pertinence to the scale dimension. Because a given scale is usually composed of an accidental hodge-podge of the possibilities, it has usually been difficult to comprehend just what model rationalizes or might rationalize a measure, and how optimally variance cancellation is being employed. However, in the study of ways in which score equivocality comes about, recognition of the existence of suppression effects is a first step toward improved usage of these cancellations.

The general problem of reducing score equivocality is a large one, imperfectly understood, and with only the fuzzy beginnings of a solution available. It cannot be discussed more than superficially in these last pages. Recent relevant contributions, however, include Meehl's suggestion for configural scoring (Meehl,

1950); the use of moderator variables by Saunders (1956) and Ghiselli (1963); Guttman's scaling technique as assisted toward practicality and nonobviousness by the Stouffer, Borgatta, Hays, and Henry (1952) suggestion of "derived-items"; and the use of multidimensional psychological criteria for the selection of items so that an item may be endorsed only when the several psychological dimensions interactively expressed by these special items all coincide in a respondent.[18] For a most thoughtful and constructive essay on the requiredness of enlisting psychological theory if psychometric accomplishments are desired, the reader is referred to the monograph by Loevenger (1957). My only intention here is to draw attention to the need for imaginative proposals and inquisitive analyses dedicated to discovering new ways of purifying, stabilizing, and disguising inventory measurement.

MORE INTENSIVE AND EXTENSIVE EMPIRICAL ANALYSES

One of the compelling attractions of structured personality inventories is the ease with which data may be collected through the procedure. Although this convenience feature may be abused, it is usually worthwhile to include a personality inventory in a research program if only for the independent evidential support it may provide or the ramifications and leads it may develop. At the same time, however, the investigator has the responsibility of seeing that his use of the inventory and its scales contributes both substantially and cumulatively to the field. Often in the past, this responsibility has not been met—perhaps because of the excessive

[18] This last approach is exemplified by the *NOC* and *NUC* scales I developed in 1955 and which are listed in Dahlstrom and Welsh (1960). The *NOC* scale is composed of items each of which expresses the interaction of overcontrol with a susceptibility to anxiety; the *NUC* scale contains items each reflecting the interaction of under-control with a personal vulnerability. Theoretically (and to a large extent in practice also), a high score is earned on these scales if and only if the respondent is *both* susceptible to anxiety *and* the possessor of the required ego-control mode. Low scores on these scales indicate the subject is *either* not a brittle character *or* has an alternative ego-control style *or* both of these. The *NOC* scale appears to index the tendency to rigidify under stress; the *NUC* scale the tendency to respond diffusely and chaotically when under pressure. The two scales are almost orthogonal to each other in a variety of samples.

data-processing labors involved in establishing the quality and special merit of a new scale. Now that the necessary computer programs have evolved, we have available solid-state genies to carry out the most monstrous clerical tasks.

Accordingly, we should now expect that no new inventory scale need find its way into the literature without careful item selection and appropriate statistical properties. With the advent of the computer, various kinds of elegance in scale construction have now become practical for the first time; potentially important item or scale statistics may be evaluated where previously the cost and sheer dullness of the human labor required turned the investigator away from these explorations. There is no longer any reason for freezing a scale into use prior to adequate scale refinement.

A further consequence of computer availability is that the correlational properties of new scales can now be studied and made known at the time the scale is offered in the literature. If this policy had been followed—at least in regard to a few "marker" or reference scales—many of the approximately 250 MMPI scales which have proliferated through the literature would have added more cumulative knowledge to the criterion-significance of the relatively few primary MMPI dimensions. A salutary contribution of the response-set controversy surrounding the MMPI is the far greater knowledge we now enjoy of the internal correlational structure of its scales.

And finally, because it is easy to collect or gain access to inventory protocols and because computer scoring of inventories is cheap and flexibly implemented, we may now anticipate analyses of scale properties and scale efficacy on larger samples and on varied samples before formal introduction of the measure. Research findings bounce around a good deal as a function of both simple sampling fluctuations and significant relational differences as the populations sampled are varied. In the past, there has been a great lag between the initial appearance of a scale and a full perspective on its merits. Now, with the computer as servant, there is no reason for this loss of time and perhaps misled research effort. When a new scale is constructed, it may be scored immediately on previously accumulated samples and its norms, predictive utility, and correlational functioning established immediately in a range of samples.

Although there has been appreciable recognition of the glistening analytical possibilities afforded by the computer, I believe the pace toward these golden resources can be quicker. With intelligent usage of the moronic labors of the computer, the structured personality inventory can enter a new era because the inertial problem of response-processing has become essentially trivial.

STRENGTHENING SCALE VALIDATION

The reason for structured personality inventories, and the measure of their usefulness, lies in the independent behaviors, outcomes, and criteria these inventories may be able to predict. A poignantly appealing item pool, splendid Kuder-Richardson reliabilities and sober scale norms avail us nothing if relationships beyond the inventory in proper number and kind cannot be found. So, when all is said and done, scale validity is the goal we seek.

In the MMPI and similar inventories, the principal method of scale construction has been to define two criterion-groups and analyze the differential frequency of response to a set of inventory items. The distinguishing items are defined as a scale to be tested and refined subsequently in comparisons of further groups meeting these criteria. Thus, the MMPI *Sc* scale was developed by contrasting a group of schizophrenics with a group of presumed normal subjects. Development of the *Pt* scale was initiated by contrasting a group of patients characterized as psychasthenic again against a group of normals (an internal consistency analysis of item-total correlations was later applied). The *Sc* and *Pt* scales so derived proved afterward to correlate at extraordinarily high levels (in the range of .8 and .9). That is, by contrasting each psychiatric subgroup against a normal sample, the scales had not been protected against the possibility of functional overlap.

Given the aspiration solely of identifying subjects with psychopathology, this failure to discriminate between the *Sc* and *Pt* scales is not too important. But when differential diagnosis be-

tween psychosis and neurosis is at issue, the high degree of correspondence between these two scales is embarrassing. Clinicians
have sometimes attempted to interpret the difference between the
Sc and *Pt* scores as indicative of the individual's inclination toward the one or the other category, but these extrapolations are
risky given the very low reliability of the differences used as a
basis for decision.

The obvious next analytical step in this situation, which to my
knowledge has never been taken, is to contrast a group of schizophrenics with a group of psychasthenics (neurotics), to identify
discriminating items and thus have a scale to provide the needed
further separation. All that is required is item analyses on several
samples, a task that at one time was a protracted one but now
occupies a computer for only seconds.

The general logical principle here may be called "successive
keying" and requires the construction of a "logical tree" of scales.
Diagnosis, categorization, or identification of the qualities of an
individual would rely on the successive application (or scoring)
of a set of scales, each scale responding pointedly to the diagnostic dilemma existing at a branch point. Thus, a first scale could
identify the existence of psychopathology; one second level scale
would further separate maladjusted persons into those who are
psychotic and those who are neurotic while another second level
scale perhaps might attempt further distinctions among the
adjusted subsample. Third level scales might distinguish among
types of psychosis, types of neurosis, and so on. The procedure is
not profound but it can provide—if the item pool has the
capability—scales specifically addressed to questions of differential diagnosis and hence the improvement of inventory validity.
Presently, single scales are asked to answer a number of questions
simultaneously and may not respond to any in an optimal fashion.[19]

Another useful approach to validity improvement depends on

[19] Rosen (1962) recently has reported a related approach. He developed
some MMPI scales by contrasting homogeneous clinical groups against
psychiatric patients-in-general. His work is a significant step in the direction
of successive keying but does not proceed as far as, I believe, the approach
might go, *e.g.*, by contrasting one homogeneous clinical group versus another
homogeneous clinical group.

the present facility of item-analytic procedures. The item-analysis method, applied across several samples or employing various and complex selection criteria for constituting contrast groups, is a most powerful technique which deserves more popular employment. The sense of a construct or the characteristics of a group can be developed by resourcefully selected comparisons against a variety of different groupings of subjects. Each contrast highlights a new facet of understanding although each is insufficient to convey the dimensional scope of the honed stone. Thus, there are many inventory items discriminating between male over-controllers and female over-controllers. These items may be distinguishing because of sex difference per se or because ego-control patterns are a function of sex-role. By contrasting male and female under-controllers, and males-in-general with females-in-general, and over-controllers of both sexes against under-controllers of both sexes, we may elucidate the bases of the differences obtained. These analyses, now so casually available, enrich our understanding of masculinity-femininity and ego-control as manifested in personality inventories and, most particularly, reveal the existence and quality of an interaction between these two dimensions. My point here is not the special merit of these findings but rather to exemplify how a variety of contrasts led by theoretical inclination, curiosity, or the stubborn motivation to systematize and unconfound analyses can provide core sets of differentiating items and hence more valid (and more subtle) scales.

Both of the foregoing approaches rely upon the existence and independent specification of subject groups possessing criterion characteristics. Whatever usefulness they may prove to have, the essential starting point of these and other analytical procedures focusing upon validity enhancement is the existence of criterion groups. The great contribution of the MMPI and related inventories has been to recognize external criteria as the beginning basis and the ultimate end of scale validity. From this recognition has come an emphasis on empiricism in scale construction. Although this empiricism has not been without its faults—recognized more readily retrospectively than prospectively—this orientation has yielded unquestionable dividends.

The validation of a scale is a process involving spiraling, reciprocal interplay between scale and criterion, theory and empiricism. On balance, I believe the MMPI has measured up well. The final triumph of the MMPI against the challenge of a response-set reinterpretation may be seen to derive from this homely and homing concern with empirical anchor points.

BIBLIOGRAPHY

Adorno, T. W., Frenkel-Brunswik, Else, Levinson, D. J., & Sanford, R. M. *The authoritarian personality.* New York: Harper & Row, 1950.

Bakan, D. A generalization of Sidman's results on group and individual functions and a criterion. *Psychol. Bull.,* 1954, *51,* 63–64.

Barnes, E. H. Factors, response bias, and the MMPI. *J. consult Psychol.,* 1956, *20,* 419–421. (a)

Barnes, E. H. Response bias and the MMPI. *J. consult. Psychol.,* 1956, *20,* 371–374. (b)

Barron, F. An ego-strength scale which predicts response to psychotherapy. *J. consult. Psychol.,* 1953, *17,* 327–333.

Bass, B. M. Authoritarianism or acquiescence. *J. abnorm. soc. Psychol.,* 1955, *51,* 616–623.

Block, J. An experimental investigation of the construct of ego-control. Unpublished Ph.D. dissertation, Stanford Univer., 1950.

Block, J. On the number of significant findings to be expected from chance. *Psychometrika,* 1960, *25,* 369–380.

Block, J. *The Q-sort method in personality assessment and psychiatric research.* Springfield, Ill.: Charles C. Thomas, 1961.

Block, J. & Bailey, D. E. Q-sort item analyses of a number of MMPI scales. *Technical Memorandum* OERL TM-55-7, Maxwell Air Force Base, Alabama: Officer Education Research Laboratory, May, 1955.

Block, J. & Bailey, D. E. A cluster analysis of 82 inventory measures of personality, interest and intellect. *IPAR Res. Monogr.,* 1955.

Block, J. & Block, Jeanne H. An investigation of the relationship between intolerance of ambiguity and ethnocentrism. *J. Pers.,* 1951, *19,* 303–311.

Block, J. & Thomas, H. Is satisfaction with self a measure of adjustment? *J. aborm. soc. Psychol.,* 1955, *51,* 254–259.

Block, J. & Turula, Emily. Identification, ego-control and adjustment. *Child Develpm.,* 1963, *34,* 945–953.

Block, Jeanne H. An experimental study of a topological representation of ego-structure. Unpublished doctoral dissertation, Stanford Univer., 1951.

Block, Jeanne H. & Block, J. An interpersonal experiment on reactions to authority. *Hum. Relat.*, 1952, *5*, 91–98.

Block, Jeanne H. & Martin, B. Predicting the behavior of children under frustration. *J. abnorm. soc. Psychol.*, 1955, *51*, 281–285.

Brackbill, G. & Little, K. B. MMPI correlates of the Taylor scale of manifest anxiety. *J. consult. Psychol.*, 1954, *18*, 433–436.

Carroll, J. B. The nature of the data, or how to choose a correlation coefficient. *Psychometrika*, 1961, *26*, 347–372.

Cattell, R. B. & Stice, G. F. *The sixteen personality factor questionnaire.* (3rd. ed.) Champaign, Ill.: Institute for Personality and Ability Testing, 1962.

Chapman, L. J. & Campbell, D. T. Response set in the *F* Scale. *J. abnorm. soc. Psychol.*, 1957, *54*, 129–132.

Christie, R., Havel, Joan, & Seidenberg, B. Is the *F* Scale irreversible? *J. abnorm. soc. Psychol.*, 1958, *56*, 143–159.

Cody, V. M. The estimation of juvenile incorrigibility. *Juv. Delinqu. Monogr.*, 1923, No. 2.

Cofer, C. N., Chance, June, & Judson, A. J. A study of malingering on the MMPI. *J. Psychol.*, 1949, *27*, 491–499.

Cohn, T. S. The relation of the *F* Scale to a response set to answer positively. *Amer. Psychologist*, 1953, *8*, 335. (Abstract)

Comrey, A. L. A factor analysis of items on the MMPI Hypochondriasis scale. *Educ. psychol. Measmt*, 1957, *17*, 568–577. (a)

Comrey, A. L. A factor analysis of items on the MMPI Depression scale. *Educ. psychol. Measmt*, 1957, *17*, 578–585. (b)

Comrey, A. L. A factor analysis of items on the MMPI Hysteria scale. *Educ. psychol. Measmt*, 1957, *17*, 586–592. (c)

Comrey, A. L. A factor analysis of items on the MMPI Psychopathic Deviate scale. *Educ. psychol. Measmt*, 1958, *18*, 91–98. (a)

Comrey, A. L. A factor analysis of items on the MMPI Paranoia scale. *Educ. psychol. Measmt*, 1958, *18*, 99–107. (b)

Comrey, A. L. A factor analysis of items on the MMPI Psychasthenia scale. *Educ. psychol. Measmt*, 1958, *18*, 293–300. (c)

Comrey, A. L. A factor analysis of items on the *F* Scale of the MMPI. *Educ. psychol. Measmt*, 1958, *18*, 621–632. (d)

Comrey, A. L. A factor analysis of items on the *K* Scale of the MMPI *Educ. psychol. Measmt*, 1958, *18*, 633–639. (e)

Comrey, A. L. & Levonian, E. A comparison of three point co-efficients in factor analysis of MMPI items. *Educ. psychol. Measmt*, 1958, *18*, 739–755.

Couch, A. & Keniston, K. Yea-sayers and nay-sayers: agreeing response set as a personality variable. *J. abnorm. soc. Psychol.*, 1960, *60*, 151–174.

Couch, A. & Keniston, K. Agreeing response set and social desirability. *J. abnorm. soc. Psychol.*, 1961, *62*, 175–179.

Cronbach, L. J. An experimental comparison of the multiple true-false and multiple multiple-choice tests. *J. educ. Psychol.*, 1941, *32*, 533–543.

Cronbach, L. J. Studies of acquiescence as a factor in the true-false test. *J. educ. Psychol.*, 1942, *33*, 401–415.

Cronbach, L. J. Response sets and test validity. *Educ. psychol. Measmt,* 1946, *6*, 475–494.

Cronbach, L. J. Further evidence on response sets and test design. *Educ. psychol. Measmt,* 1950, *10*, 3–31.

Crowne, D. P. & Marlowe, D. A new scale of social desirability independent of psychopathology. *J. consult. Psychol.*, 1960, *24*, 349–354.

Dahlstrom, W. G. & Welsh, G. S. *An MMPI handbook.* Minneapolis: Univer. of Minnesota Press, 1960.

Drake, L. E. A social I. E. scale for the MMPI. *J. appl. Psychol.*, 1946, *30*, 51–54.

Edwards, A. L. The relationship between the judged desirability of a trait and the probability that the trait will be endorsed. *J. appl. Psychol.*, 1953, *37*, 90–93.

Edwards, A. L. *The social desirability variable in personality assessment and research.* New York: Dryden, 1957.

Edwards, A. L. Social desirability and personality test construction. In B. M. Bass & I. A. Berg (Eds.), *Objective approaches to personality assessment.* New York: Van Nostrand, 1959.

Edwards, A. L. Social desirability or acquiescence in the MMPI? A case study with the SD scale. *J. abnorm. soc. Psychol.*, 1961, *63*, 351–359.

Edwards, A. L. Personal communication. August 29, 1962; September 21, 1962.

Edwards, A. L., Diers, Carol J., & Walker, J. N. Response sets and factor loadings on 61 personality scales. *J. appl. Psychol.*, 1962, *46*, 220–225.

Edwards, A. L., Gocka, E. F., & Holloway, H. The development of an MMPI acquiescence scale. *J. clin. Psychol.*, 1964, *20*, 148–150.

Edwards, A. L. & Heathers, Louise B. The first factor of the MMPI: social desirability or ego-strength. *J. consult. Psychol.*, 1962, *26*, 99–100.

Edwards, A. L., Heathers, Louise B., & Fordyce, W. E. Correlations of new MMPI scales with Edwards' SD scale. *J. clin. Psychol.*, 1960, *16*, 26–29.

Edwards, A. L. & Walker, J. N. A note on the Couch and Keniston measure of agreement response set. *J. abnorm. soc. Psychol.*, 1961, 62, 173–174. (a)

Edwards, A. L. & Walker, J. N. Social desirability and agreement response set. *J. abnorm. soc. Psychol.*, 1961, 62, 180–183. (b)

Edwards, A. L. & Walker, J. N. A short form of the MMPI: The SD scale. *Psychol. Reps.*, 1961, 8, 485–486. (c)

Edwards, A. L. & Walsh, J. A. The relationship between the intensity of the social desirability keying of a scale and the correlation of the scale with Edwards' SD scale and the first factor loading of the scale. *J. clin. Psychol.*, 1963, 19, 200–203.

Estes, W. K. The problem of inferences from curves based on group data. *Psychol. Bull.*, 1956, 53, 134–141.

Eysenck, H. J. *The structure of human personality.* New York: Wiley, 1953.

Foster, R. J. Acquiescent response set as a measure of acquiescence. *J. abnorm. soc. Psychol.*, 1961, 63, 155–160.

Foster, R. J. & Grigg, A. E. Acquiescent response set as a measure of acquiescence: Further evidence. *J. abnorm. soc. Psychol.*, 1963, 67, 304–306.

Fricke, B. G. A response bias (B) scale for the MMPI. *J. counsel. Psychol.*, 1957, 4, 149–153.

Gage, N. L. & Chatterjee, B. B. The psychological meaning of acquiescence set: Further evidence. *J. abnorm. soc. Psychol.*, 1960, 60, 280–283.

Gage, N. L., Leavitt, G. S., & Stone, G. C. The psychological meaning of acquiescence set for authoritarianism. *J. abnorm. soc. Psychol.*, 1957, 55, 98–103.

Ghiselli, E. E. Moderating effects and differential reliability and validity. *J. appl. Psychol.*, 1963, 47, 81–86.

Goldberg, L. R. & Rorer, L. G. Test-retest item statistics for original and reversed MMPI items. *Oregon Res. Inst. Res. Monogr.*, 3, No. 1. Eugene: Oregon Research Institute, 1963.

Gough, H. G. A new dimension of status: I. Development of a personality scale. *Amer. sociol. Rev.*, 1948, 13, 401–409.

Gough, H. G. Studies of social intolerance: II. A personality scale for anti-Semitism. *J. soc. Psychol.*, 1951, 33, 247–255.

Gough, H. G. Predicting social participation. *J. soc. Psychol.*, 1952, 35, 227–233.

Gough, H. G. Special keys developed for the MMPI. Unpublished manuscript, Univer. of California, Berkeley, 1952.

Gough, H. G. A nonintellectual intelligence test. *J. consult. Psychol.*, 1953, 17, 242–246.

Gough, H. G., McClosky, H., & Meehl, P. E. A personality scale for dominance. *J. abnorm. soc. Psychol.*, 1951, *46*, 360–366.

Gough, H. G., McKee, M. G., & Yandell, R. J. Adjective checklist analyses of a number of selected psychometric and assessment variables. *Technical Memorandum* OERL TM-10, Maxwell Air Force Base, Alabama: Officer Education Research Laboratory, May, 1955.

Green, B. F. Attitude measurement. In G. Lindzey (Ed.), *Handbook of social psychology*, Vol. I. Cambridge, Mass.: Addison-Wesley, 1954.

Guilford, J. P. & Guilford, Ruth B. Personality factors D, R, T and A. *J. abnorm. soc. Psychol.*, 1939, *34*, 21–36.

Guttman, L. The principal components of scale analysis. In S. A. Stouffer *et al.*, *Measurement and prediction*. Princeton, N. J.: Princeton Univer. Press, 1950. Pp. 312–361.

Hanley, C. Social desirability and response bias in the MMPI. *J. consult. Psychol.*, 1961, *25*, 13–20.

Harris, R. E. Personal communication. September 17, 1962.

Harris, R. E. & Lingoes, J. C. Subscales for the MMPI: An aid to profile interpretation. Unpublished manuscript, The Langley Porter Neuropsychiatric Inst., 1st. & Parnassus Aves., San Francisco 22, Calif., 1955.

Hathaway, S. R. & Meehl, P. E. *An atlas for the clinical use of the MMPI*. Minneapolis: Univer. of Minnesota Press, 1951.

Heineman, C. E. A forced-choice form of the Taylor Anxiety Scale. Unpublished doctoral dissertation, State Univer. of Iowa, 1952.

Jackson, D. N. Stylistic response determinants in the California Psychological Inventory. *Educ. psychol. Measmt*, 1960, *20*, 339–346.

Jackson, D. N. & Messick, S. J. A note on ethnocentrism and acquiescent response sets. *J. abnorm. soc. Psychol.*, 1957, *54*, 132–134.

Jackson, D. N. & Messick, S. J. Content and style in personality assessment. *Psychol. Bull.*, 1958, *55*, 243–252.

Jackson, D. N. & Messick, S. J. Acquiescence and desirability as response determinants on the MMPI. *Educ. psychol. Measmt*, 1961, *21*, 771–792.

Jackson, D. N. & Messick, S. J. Response styles on the MMPI: comparison of clinical and normal samples. *J. abnorm. soc. Psychol.*, 1962, *65*, 285–299.

Kaiser, H. The varimax criterion for analytic rotation in factor analysis. *Psychometrika*, 1958, *23*, 187–200.

Kassebaum, G. G., Couch, A. S., & Slater, P. E. The factorial dimensions of the MMPI. *J. consult. Psychol.*, 1959, *23*, 226–236.

Leavitt, H. J., Hax, H., & Rouche, J. H. "Authoritarianism" and agreement with things authoritative. *J. Psychol.*, 1955, *40*, 215–221.

Lentz, T. F. Acquiescence as a factor in the measurement of personality. *Psychol. Bull.*, 1938, *35*, 659. (Abstract)

Lingoes, J. C. MMPI factors of the Harris and the Wiener subscales. *J. consult. Psychol.*, 1960, *24*, 74–83.

Little, K. B. & Fisher, J. Two new experimental scales of the MMPI. *J. consult. Psychol.*, 1958, *22*, 305–306.

Loevenger, Jane. Objective tests as instruments of psychological theory. *Psychol. Reps.*, 1957, *3*, 635–694.

Lorge, I. Gen-like: Halo or reality? *Psychol. Bull.*, 1937, *34*, 545–546.

McGee, R. K. The relationship between response styles and personality variables: I. The measurement of response acquiescence. *J. abnorm. soc. Psychol.*, 1962, *64*, 229–233

McNemar, Q. *Psychological statistics.* New York: Wiley, 1962.

Mandler, G. Stimulus variables and subject variables: A caution. *Psychol. Rev.*, 1951, *66*, 145–149.

Meehl, P. E. Configural scoring. *J. consult. Psychol.*, 1950, *14*, 165–171.

Meehl, P. E. & Hathaway, S. R. The *K* factor as a suppressor variable in the MMPI. *J. appl. Psychol.*, 1946, *30*, 525–564.

Messick, S. Dimensions of social desirability. *J. consult Psychol.*, 1960, *24*, 279–287.

Messick, S. Response style and content measures from personality inventories. *Educ. psychol. Measmt*, 1962, *22*, 41–56.

Messick, S. & Jackson, D. N. Acquiescence and the factorial interpretation of the MMPI. *Psychol. Bull.*, 1961, *58*, 299–304. (a)

Messick, S. & Jackson, D. N. Desirability scale values and dispersions for MMPI items. *Psychol. Reps.*, 1961, *8*, 409–414. (b)

Mitchell, J. V. & Pierce-Jones, J. A factor analysis of Gough's California Psychological Inventory. *J. consult. Psychol.*, 1960, *24*, 453–456.

Mogar, R. E. Three versions of the *F* Scale and performance on the semantic differential. *J. abnorm. soc. Psychol.*, 1960, *60*, 262–265.

Nichols, R. C. & Schnell, R. R. Factor scales for the California Psychological Inventory. *J. consult. Psychol.*, 1963, *27*, 228–235.

Oettel, A. Leadership: A psychological study. Unpublished doctoral dissertation, Univer. of California, Berkeley, 1953.

Ong, J. S. L. Measurement with opposite forms of an inventory. Unpublished doctoral dissertation, Univer. of California, Berkeley, 1963.

Peabody, D. Attitude content and agreement set in scales of authoritarianism, dogmatism, antisemitism, and economic conservatism. *J. abnorm. soc. Psychol.*, 1961, *63*, 1–11.

Reichenbach, H. *The rise of scientific philosophy.* Berkeley: Univer. of California Press, 1951.

Rokeach, M. The double agreement phenomenon: Three hypotheses. *Psychol. Rev.,* 1963, *70,* 304–309.

Rorer, L. G. The function of item content in MMPI responses. Unpublished doctoral dissertation, Univer. of Minnesota, Minneapolis, 1963.

Rorer, L. G. Personal communication. January 5, 1964.

Rosen, A. Development of MMPI scales based on a reference group of psychiatric patients. *Psychol. Monogr.,* 1962, *76,* No. 8.

Sarason, I. G. Empirical findings and theoretical problems in the use of anxiety scales. *Psychol. Bull.,* 1960, *57,* 403–415.

Saunders, D. R. Moderator variables in prediction. *Educ. psychol. Measmt,* 1956, *16,* 209–222.

Schofield, W. S. MMPI response changes with certain therapies. Unpublished doctoral dissertation, Univer. of Minnesota, Minneapolis, 1948.

Sidman, M. A note on functional relations obtained from group data. *Psychol. Bull.,* 1952, *49,* 263–269.

Siller, J. & Chipman, A. Response set paralysis: Implications for measurement and control. *J. consult. Psychol.,* 1963, *27,* 432–438.

Stouffer, S. A., Borgatta, E. F., Hays, D. G., & Henry, A. F. A technique for improving cumulative scales. *Publ. Opin. Quart.,* 1952, *16,* 273–291.

Stricker, L. J. Note on social desirability response style and learning. *J. educ. Psychol.,* 1963, *54,* 52–56.

Taylor, J. B. Social desirability and MMPI performance: The individual case. *J. consult. Psychol.,* 1959, *23,* 514–517.

Taylor, Janet A. A personality scale of manifest anxiety. *J. abnorm. soc. Psychol.,* 1953, *48,* 285–290.

Taylor, Janet A. Drive theory and manifest anxiety. *Psychol. Bull.,* 1956, *53,* 303–320.

Thorndike, E. L. On the fallacy of imputing the correlation found for groups to the individual or smaller groups composing them. *Amer. J. Psychol.,* 1939, *52,* 122–124.

Tyler, F. T. A factorial analysis of fifteen MMPI scales. *J. consult. Psychol.,* 1951, *15,* 541–546.

Welsh, G. S. Factor dimensions A and R. In G. S. Welsh & W. G. Dahlstrom (Eds.), *Basic readings on the MMPI in Psychology and medicine.* Minneapolis: Univer. of Minnesota Press, 1956.

Wheeler, W. M., Little, K. B., & Lehner, G. F. J. The internal structure of the MMPI. *J. consult. Psychol.,* 1951, *15,* 134–141.

Wiggins, J. S. Interrelationships among MMPI measures of dissimulation under standard and social desirability instructions. *J. consult. Psychol.*, 1959, *23*, 419–427.

Wiggins, J. S. Strategic, method, and stylistic variance in the MMPI. *Psychol. Bull.*, 1962, *59*, 224–242.

Wiggins, J. S. & Rumrill, C. Social desirability in the MMPI and Welsh's factor scales *A* and *R*. *J. consult. Psychol.*, 1959, *23*, 100–106.

Woodworth, R. S. *Woodworth's personal data sheet.* Chicago: C. H. Stoelting Co., 1918.

Wrigley, C. & Neuhaus, J. O. The matching of two sets of factors. *Contract Memorandum Report*, A-32, Urbana, Ill.: Univer. of Illinois, 1955. P. 13.

APPENDIX A

The MMPI *ER-O* Scale: Its Definition, Some Norms, and Its Correlations with Selected MMPI Scales

The MMPI *ER-O* scale is composed of 108 items related to the first or Alpha factor of the MMPI. The criterion groups were composed of individuals earning extreme factor scores on the Alpha dimension (95 Alpha Highs versus 97 Alpha Lows, selected from a total of 400 subjects). The keyed responses are evenly divided between "trues" and "falses" to prevent the intrusion of an acquiescence interpretation.

The item numbers of the "true"-keyed portion of the *ER-O* scale are: 3, 7, 8, 9, 18, 55, 57, 63, 78, 79, 103, 107, 122, 130, 137, 152, 153, 155, 160, 163, 169, 173, 176, 187, 190, 207, 214, 230, 243, 257, 262, 264, 274, 281, 302, 309, 318, 353, 367, 371, 379, 399, 401, 407, 412, 429, 462, 464, 479, 521, 527, 533, 542, and 547.

The item numbers of the "false"-keyed portion of the *ER-O* scale are: 13, 15, 21, 26, 27, 29, 31, 32, 34, 39, 40, 41, 43, 44, 47, 52, 61, 62, 72, 76, 84, 86, 93, 94, 97, 108, 109, 114, 117, 124, 125, 129, 135, 138, 139, 142, 147, 148, 156, 157, 158, 161, 162, 166, 182, 186, 189, 215, 216, 217, 224, 226, 234, and 236.

For Samples A through I, described earlier, the *means* on the *ER-O* scale are: 89.46, 88.69, 85.74, 81.89, 80.20, 59.72, 72.84, 82.78, and 66.01.

For the same nine samples, the *standard deviations* of the *ER-O* scale are: 10.14, 9.87, 9.16, 13.57, 15.10, 18.23. 13.67, 10.78, and 16.34.

The Kuder-Richardson Formula 20 *reliabilities* for the *ER-O* scale within Samples A through I are: .89, .86, .83, .92, .93, .94, .90, .87, and .93.

We have chosen to report the correlations of *ER-O* with only a few, selected MMPI scales: *SD, Pt, ER-S,* and *EC-5* (a measure of the second and orthogonal factor of the MMPI—see Appendix B).

The correlations (uncorrected for attenuation) of *ER-O* with the *SD* scale are: .80, .74, .80, .90, .89, .92, .88, .87, and .85.

The correlations (uncorrected for attenuation) of *ER-O* with the *Pt* scale are: −.83, −.81, −.87, −.90, −.93, −.91, −.85, −.85, and −.90.

The correlations (uncorrected for attenuation) of *ER-O* with the *ER-S* scale are: .69, .70, .73, .81, .82, .66, .68, .65, and .60. There is no item overlap between these obvious and subtle measures of the ER dimension.

The correlations (uncorrected for attenuation) of *ER-O* with the *EC-5* scale are .34, .21, .09, .15, .18, −.11, .29, .10, and .15.

The MMPI *EC-5* Scale: Its Definition, Some Norms, and Its Correlation with Selected MMPI Scales

The MMPI *EC-5* scale is composed of 32 items related to the second or Beta factor of the MMPI. The criterion groups were composed of individuals of both sexes who earned extreme factor scores on the Beta dimension (97 Beta Highs versus 98 Beta Lows, selected from a total of 400 subjects). The keyed responses are evenly divided between "trues" and "falses" to prevent the intrusion of an acquiescence interpretation.

The item numbers of the "true"-keyed portion of the *EC-5* scale are: 37, 74, 95, 96, 111, 132, 133, 294, 329, 373, 377, 453, 466, 490, 503, and 548.

The item numbers of the "false"-keyed portion of the *EC-5* scale are: 38, 45, 56, 118, 195, 208, 215, 372, 415, 430, 434, 446, 447, 482, 491, and 537.

For Samples A through I, described earlier, the *means* on the *EC-5* scale are: 11.73, 15.06, 14.20, 19.79, 19.53, 14.41, 19.34, 17.25, and 19.74.

For the same nine samples, the *standard deviations* of the *EC-5* scale are: 3.51, 4.66, 4.72, 3.12, 4.00, 4.37, 3.42, 4.61, and 4.05.

The Kuder-Richardson Formula 20 *reliabilities* for the *EC-5* scale, within Samples A through I, are: .62, .74, .76, .46, .68, .65, .53, .76, and .65.

The correlations of *EC-5* with the *ER-O* scale have been reported in Appendix A.

The correlations (uncorrected for attenuation) of *EC-5* with Welsh's *R* scale are: .49, .46, .55, .46, .33, .47, .12, .65, and .40.

The correlations (uncorrected for attenuation) of *EC-5* with the *Ma* scale are: −.40, −.40, −.26, −.24, −.53, −.31, −.28, −.54, and −.36.

There appear to be differences between the sexes in the way ego-control is manifested and, within the constraints of the MMPI, it will be useful to employ sex-specific *EC* scales. The scales, *EC-5M* and *EC-5F*, are designed for males and females, respectively, and derive from analyses of Beta Highs and Beta Lows for the sexes treated separately. For *EC-5M*, the desideratum of a balance between "trues" and "falses" had to be abandoned; for *EC-5F*, the balance is essentially maintained (18–16) but the scale is rather short. These scales should be viewed as preliminary—not final—efforts toward improving the validity of representation of the EC dimension by recognizing sex differences.

The "true"-keyed items of *EC-5M* are: 58, 82, 111, 115, 133, 171, 172, 180, 201, 249, 267, 292, 304, 321, 329, 377, 378, 385, 453, 503, 509, and 548.

The "false"-keyed items of *EC-5M* are: 19, 21, 38, 39, 45, 56, 57, 78, 99, 118, 126, 142, 145, 149, 181, 204, 208, 229, 231, 233, 234, 238, 254, 277, 282, 322, 400, 417, 425, 426, 430, 432, 438, 441, 446, 447, 449, 450, 451, 452, 463, 465, 471, 482, 520, 521, 529, and 547.

The "true"-keyed items of *EC-5F* are: 55, 68, 82, 111, 117, 124, 141, 171, 180, 201, 260, 267, 292, 304, 316, 321, 377, and 530.

The "false"-keyed items of *EC-5F* are: 21, 57, 126, 204, 208, 226, 309, 409, 428, 429, 432, 479, 482, 521, 523, and 529.

For the male samples, Samples A, B, C, and F, the *means* on the *EC-5M* scale are: 30.39, 34.73, 32.67, and 34.26. The *standard deviations* for these four samples are: 8.46, 9.26, 10.86, and 9.10. The K-R Formula 20 *reliabilities* are: .84, .85, .89, and .82.

For the female samples, Samples D, E, G, H, and I, the *means* on the *EC-5F* scale are: 14.21, 14.43, 15.11, 14.46, and 16.10. The *standard deviations* for these five samples are: 5.36, 6.78, 4.75, 5.54, and 5.37. The K-R Formula 20 *reliabilities* are: .78, .87, .69, .79, and .75.

It will be observed that higher K-R Formula 20 reliabilities are achieved by separate sex-specific *EC* scales than are developed by the less particular *EC-5* scale.